Peter Shaw has an extensive background in drama both in and outside of church life. Currently Senior Publications Editor for Tearfund England, Peter edits and writes for Tearfund's flagship publication, *Tear Times*, and Tearfund's Prayer Diary. Peter also writes drama sketches for Tearfund's church packs, as well as writing and producing Tearfund's annual Christmas church pack and appeal.

He has a Masters Degree in Playwriting from Goldsmiths College, and has had a number of plays performed, including a piece selected for the 2001 International Playwriting Festival at the Warehouse Theatre in Croydon and a romantic comedy, *Love at First*, which toured in Surrey and West London in 2002 and was revived for the 2003 Edinburgh Fringe Festival. Peter is the author of *Beyond the Cringe* (Kevin Mayhew, 2005) and *All-Age Sketches for the Christian Year* (Barnabas, 2006).

GW00458411

Barnabas
for
Children®

Barnabas for Children® is a registered word mark and the logo is a registered device mark of
The Bible Reading Fellowship.
Text copyright © Peter Shaw 2012
The author asserts the moral right
to be identified as the author of this work

Published by
The Bible Reading Fellowship
15 The Chambers, Vineyard
Abingdon OX14 3FE
United Kingdom
Tel: +44 (0)1865 319700
Email: enquiries@brf.org.uk
Website: www.brf.org.uk
BRF is a Registered Charity

ISBN 978 0 85746 005 9
First published 2012
10 9 8 7 6 5 4 3 2 1 0
All rights reserved

Acknowledgments

Unless otherwise stated, scripture quotations are taken from the Contemporary English
Version of the Bible published by HarperCollins Publishers, copyright © 1991, 1992, 1995
American Bible Society.

Scripture quotations taken from the Holy Bible, New International Version, copyright ©
1973, 1978, 1984 by International Bible Society. Used by permission of Hodder & Stoughton
Publishers, a member of the Hachette Livre UK Group.

Scripture quotations taken from the Holy Bible, Today's New International Version, copyright
© 2004 by International Bible Society. Used by permission of Hodder & Stoughton Publishers,
a member of the Hachette Livre UK Group.

Scripture quotations marked (NLT) are taken from the Holy Bible, New Living Translation,
copyright © 1996, 2004. Used by permission of Tyndale House Publishers, Inc., Wheaton,
Illinois 60189. All rights reserved.

'Stigma? What stigma?' Copyright Alex Mowbray, 2011. Used by kind permission.

The paper used in the production of this publication was supplied by mills that source their
raw materials from sustainably managed forests. Soy-based inks were used in its printing and
the laminate film is biodegradable.

A catalogue record for this book is available from the British Library

Printed in Singapore by Craft Print International Ltd

Drama

out of a

Crisis

20 challenging, fun and inspirational
sketches about poverty and justice

Peter Shaw

For my son, Benedict Shaw, born shortly after I finished this book.
I pray that he grows up in a world prepared to address and tackle
the problems of poverty and injustice.

And for my father, Philip 'Pip' Shaw,
who sadly died before it was published.
I miss you, Dad.

~ * ~

*

Contents

*

Foreword

Well over one billion people in our world go through every day surrounded by the reality of grinding, debilitating poverty, pressing in from every side. I would argue that there is no more pressing issue for us to engage with as followers of Jesus Christ.

However, we are frequently overwhelmed by the scale of global poverty. We ask ourselves whether we can really make a difference. And we find it very hard to move beyond statistics from half a world away, and allow the human stories, with their raw emotion, drama and authenticity, to grab our hearts and minds and move us to action.

This is where this fantastic book comes in. For many years, Peter has poured his energy, heart and creativity into bringing the stories of the poorest into our lives, homes and churches in fresh and vibrant ways. He is an authority not only on the issues that affect people living in poverty, but also on communicating these issues with power and imagination.

Just as Jesus used parables to teach and illuminate, Peter brings us close to people living in poverty through 20 brilliant drama sketches. Each one encourages us to connect more closely, reflect more deeply and act more whole-heartedly. We're taken on journeys that lead us to embrace all our emotions: shock, anger, sadness, humour, joy and hope.

I love how Peter has framed each sketch with great background colour, arresting statistics and facts, grounding scripture and very practical suggestions on what we can do next to make a real difference. He also offers simple guidance and tips, empowering us all, however inexperienced, to organise a drama sketch that engages and moves an audience to action.

Matthew Frost, Chief Executive, Tearfund

*

Introduction

For the most part, we want churches and Christian gatherings to be happy, pleasant places where we can enjoy being with God and each other. That's no bad thing—it's great that we want our events to be welcoming to all—but where does poverty fit in? Sometimes it's a discarded leaflet on a pew, a dusty collection box at the back, or an old notice on the board.

The apostle Paul says this: 'When others are happy, be happy with them, and when they are sad, be sad' (Romans 12:15). So, clearly, even when life is easy for us, we are called to seek out and share the lives of those who are suffering (as well as celebrate with those who are joyful).

For my day job, I work for Tearfund, editing two of their publications—*Tear Times* and the *Prayer Diary*—and, because of this, I'm sometimes asked by churches (or I ask them) to raise awareness of an issue or event. Maybe there's been a devastating natural disaster, or it's World AIDS Day or Tearfund have a prayer week to promote. When I stand in front of a church and begin by saying something like, 'In Africa…', I can actually see people's hearts sink a little.

I think I know why that is. It's not because people lack compassion or don't want to be confronted by world poverty. I think it's because people feel that they can't make a difference. Not everyone, of course—but remember, I'm speaking of believers who have the same 'mighty power' that Paul talks about in Ephesians 1:19.

Through my work with Tearfund, I have the privilege to visit projects and church initiatives in some of the poorest places on earth, and I can only describe the experience, on the whole, as uplifting. It's extraordinary to see God moving in powerful life-changing ways among the most overlooked and marginalised people on this planet. In fact, I believe God's presence is manifest more clearly among the poorest communities than anywhere else on earth.

That's what I want people to experience through these sketches and by raising these issues and delving a little deeper—not a feeling of guilt that we're not doing enough, but praise for God, who couldn't stand by as his children suffered; a God who became a humble man and stated his aim as being 'to tell the good news to the poor' (Luke 4:18).

Drama is an amazing tool. Jesus used parables (a performance with characters and stories) to illuminate rather than to give clear answers. I hope you will use these sketches to do the same, and that they offer an effective and enhancing way to introduce poverty and justice into your church gatherings. Like parables, though, they need to be grappled with, explored and questioned. If these short dramas encourage more people to look more closely into the problems of poverty, then the book has done its job.

When we start channelling the 'mighty power' that characterises the people of Christ to connect with God's compassion for people who live in poverty, there comes a realisation: it's not just about joining with poor communities in their struggles; it's also about rejoicing with them as they overcome their circumstances. It's a journey of discovery as we realise that, for all our wealth and opportunities, we often have a poorer experience of God. We have much to learn from those who, materially, have so little.

*

Prayer and poverty

God help us

Curtain up

Throughout the Bible we learn about God's compassion for people who live in poverty and about his anger at suffering. We also learn about one of the great mysteries: prayer. While we may not always know why or how it works, we do know that prayer is transformative.

Not only does prayer have the power to change situations; it can change our hearts. When we pray, we share in God's concerns and agree with him that we must take the lead in transforming situations. Poverty is high on God's agenda: he wants us to share his compassion for those in need and to work with him to do something about it.

Bible backdrop

'Your kingdom come, your will be done, on earth as it is in heaven.'
MATTHEW 6:10 (TNIV)

As we look at the suffering and poverty in the world, it is clear that God's will is not being done. (Perhaps that's why Jesus included this cry when giving guidelines on how to pray.) In Matthew 6:5–14, Jesus instructs his disciples about discipline in devotion, urging his followers to pray regularly and systematically.

Sermon prompt

Prayer for huge world issues such as climate change, hunger, disease and disasters is often difficult. It's not a problem so much of what to pray as where to start—and when will it end? It would be great to offer your church some helpful pointers about praying for global issues, so that people's prayer lives can become more focused and effective. It would also be good to emphasise that prayer should lead to action: how can you become part of the answer to your own prayers?

Taking it further: prayer resources

Tearfund's prayer zone is a great place to connect with Christians and churches praying for poverty and justice issues. Here you'll find the latest updates on pressing world issues and clear instructions on how to pray. You can also sign up for Tearfund's weekly prayer email, 'One Voice', find a prayer group near you and learn about Tearfund's annual week of prayer for poverty. See www.tearfund. org/praying for details, and be part of a global poverty prayer movement.

Cast

There is just one part: NEIL. The name is a play on words and is not mentioned, so the character can be played by either gender.

Staging: props, costumes and effects

Not much staging is needed. You could go to the extreme of having a bed on stage, but it's really not necessary: just bring an old pillow and a duvet and lay them on the floor. Props include a scrap of paper and a map of Milton Keynes. Any road map will do: the audience will never see!

Script: God help us

A quest to pray for poverty peters out through lack of preparation.

Scene

Late at night, NEIL is in his bedroom, sitting on the edge of his bed, ready to pray.

Neil:

(Yawns) Right, it's nearly 11.45, so I have exactly the right time left to fulfil my covenant unto the Lord. *(To himself)* Yes, you great prayer warrior, you are about to embark on a journey into prayer. Quarter of an hour every day, for a whole week, praying about poverty. *(Looks at watch)* Starting... now!

(Kneels) Dear Lord, thank you for poverty. *(Pause, composes)* Sorry, I'll start again. Father God, I pray for all the poor ones everywhere. Everywhere. Particularly the most poorest ones. Amen.

(Gets up) So that was... *(Looks at watch)* 15 seconds of solid prayer. Minus the false start. *(Pause)* Oh yes, I have this! *(Pulls a tatty sheet of notepad from pocket)* Great! 'Five top tips for praying for poverty.' Who'd have thought that the notes I took in church would come in useful? This should help fill the time.

(*Reading*) 'Point one: Don't just pray for everything, pray for something!' Good point. 'There are lots of causes of injustice and poverty around the world, like inadequate water and sanitation, climate change and HIV, so pick one and prat into it.' Prat into it? (*Looks again*) Oh, *pray* into it! Water and sanitation—not sure what that is all about... Climate change is a bit technical... (*Yawns*) HIV. That'll have to do. HIV? HIV? Yes.

(*Kneels*) Lord God, I pray for all those people with HIVs. It can't be easy driving a huge truck, often alone, late at night. Please be with all HIV drivers. Amen. (*Looks at watch*) So that's, what, two minutes? I think I still need some inspiration. What's tip two? (*Reads from paper*) 'Poverty can seem like a huge tissue.' Tissue? Oh, I think that should be *issue*. 'Poverty can seem like a huge issue, but it's hard to pray for billions or even millions of people. But it's actually individuals and families that bear the brunt of poverty. So pray directly for people affected, by name if you can.' By name? I don't think I know any. Oh, I'll just have to pray as the Lord prompts me...

(*Kneels*) Mighty God! I pray, oh Father, for my dear, dear brother... (*Thinks*) Um Bongo... who lives in the... Congo. I pray that you'll bless tropical fruit drink business. Because, when it comes to sun and fun and goodness in the jungle, we all prefer the sunny funny one they call Um Bongo. Amen.

(Gets up) Well, that could have gone a bit better, but… *(Looks at watch, yawns)* At least we're three-or-so minutes in. What's the next tip? *(Consults paper)* 'Another useful thing to have around is a mop.' A mop? Not sure my prayer life is ever going to get that messy. *(Looks again)* Oh, a *map* '… of a place affected by poverty.' Good point, that'll help me focus. Take some territory in prayer. *(Searches around)* I'm sure I had one here… *(Finds map under pillow)* Yes! Just what I needed, a map. And it just so happens this is a map of… *(checks)* Milton Keynes. Fantastic. Let us pray…

(Kneels, spreads out the map) Heavenly Father, I lift up the beleaguered folk of Milton Keynes. Lord, be with them as they navigate the complicated grid system that characterises their town. I pray that they will maintain good relations with the nearby people of Newport Pagnell. Amen.

(Gets up, yawns) Gosh, this is a struggle. *(Looks at watch)* Six minutes in and only two tips left. *(Consults paper)* Point four… 'It's a really good idea to get prepared, read up about the subject, visit a website or two…' What? It's nearly midnight! This should have been point one! Oh, I'll have to skip that… *(Looks at watch)* Still got seven minutes to go. *(Consults paper)*

Last point. 'Don't just pray, Lisbon.' Lisbon? Isn't that the capital of Portugal? *(Looks again)* Oh, *listen*! 'Meditate and reflect; search out the heart of God. What is he prompting you to pray about poverty and justice?' Good point! Let's listen to God...

(Kneels, eyes shut) Lord, I'm here; speak to me. *(Pause, yawns)* Maybe if I just get myself a bit comfy, I'll hear him better. *(Crawls under the bedclothes)* I'm still listening, Lord. *(Pause)* Still listening... *(snores long and loud)*.

END

Poem: A wing and

Sticking with the theme of prayer and poverty, here's a poem to help you reflect (and provide a contrast to the sketch). The poem could also be performed by including mimed actions to illustrate the lines.

I see a world in full bleed
Steeped in hunger and greed
No comic relief
Just children in need

And parents living in fear
For year after year, after year

Old people working
Young people unemployed
Their livelihoods destroyed
With no hope to fill the void

A scarred earth,
Resources stripped,
The poor getting poorer and
The rich staying rich

And I see my own hope to change it
To play my part and rearrange it
But I'm too small to make it big
An insignificant twig
In a forest of poverty
And it's that that bothers me

Not that the need is too great
But that I'm not great enough,
And while it's easy to scoff
I find it hard to shake off
The niggling feeling things aren't right
And just get on with my life

While ignorance is surely bliss,
I surely can't ignore this

So what to do?
Potter on, shuffle off
And hope that what I do is enough
To please a God whose justice
Just isn't possible to achieve
By little, poor old me?

If only there was a way
A mechanism, say,
To cry out and be heard
And make a difference in this world

A way of asking, pleading, crying
On behalf of those who are dying
A shout out for those
Whose lives are in the throes
Of hunger, disease and death
For them I'd spare a breath
A whole lungful of air
And I'd call this pleading, prayer
And I'd do it every day
Until poverty goes away

*

Food security

Nothing in the fridge

Curtain up

Across the world, more than 900 million people are experiencing
extreme hunger, and, sadly, that figure is on the increase. World
food prices are soaring and 'food security' is a phrase that we need
to hear about more often. The World Food Summit of 1996 defined
food security as existing 'when all people at all times have access
to sufficient, safe, nutritious food to maintain a healthy and active
life'. So a lack of food security is when people don't have enough
good, nourishing food, leaving them ill and inactive. Nearly a
billion people are in that desperate position and, as the climate
changes, the figure is set to rise.

Bible backdrop

Give your food to the hungry and care for the homeless. Then
your light will shine in the dark; your darkest hour will be like the
noonday sun.
ISAIAH 58:10

When Christians are confronted by others about hunger, they are
often asked why God does not feed starving people. Doesn't he
care? The answer is that the earth is richly resourced with enough
food for everyone, and God calls on us, as good stewards of the
earth, to share this abundance fairly. As Christians, we need to be

in the forefront of providing food security for all—not just feeding those who are hungry but also giving them the knowledge, skills and opportunities to feed themselves, and removing restrictions that prevent them from doing so.

Sermon prompt

This sketch was written for Tearfund's harvest church resources in 2010, called 'One Family'. It told the story of a family in Cambodia—Mol, Tol and their four children—who were struggling to grow enough food to feed themselves. Thanks to Tearfund's partner WDO, the family have learnt much more about agriculture and growing sustainable food. But the sketch has much broader themes about how richly we are blessed (and we don't recognise it), and how little food many families have to cope with.

Keeping allotments and growing food in the back garden is an activity that's becoming more and more popular in the UK. While that's a really great thing, we're unlikely to starve if our potato crop is blighted. (24-hour supermarkets are not an endangered species just yet.) For many millions across the world, growing food is neither a hobby nor a pleasurable pastime; it is a matter of life and death.

You may find that some people in your congregation are cynical about traditional 'aid' (and you might share some of their concerns). That's why it is important to raise the message about food security—about giving people the skills, equipment and opportunity to feed themselves sustainably. In that way, providing food security is more like the feeding of the 5000 in Matthew 14: when we offer the resources we have, God can multiply and greatly increase the yield, feeding far more than our small sacrifice alone could supply.

Taking it further: 'Connected church'

As mentioned above, some people find it difficult to understand how giving can be effective and rewarding. When churches have a direct link with a project overseas, it makes giving and prayer much more meaningful. Through Tearfund's 'Connected church' you can have the benefit of a direct relationship with a church-based project in a poor community. You can decide which of the projects you want to support, develop an enriching, mutually beneficial relationship and see lives transformed through putting God's compassion into action. Visit www.tearfund.org/connectedchurch for more details.

Cast

There are only two cast members, MAN and WOMAN. With a few tweaks, however, this script could be about any gender combination—the relationship changed from a married couple to two friends sharing a home, or mother and son, and so on.

Staging: props, costumes and effects

A sofa or something similar is quite important to the set. A fridge would be good (you probably have one in the church kitchen), but it might prove problematic to shift, so you could mime a fridge instead. (Put some removable tape down to mark where the 'invisible' fridge is.)

Script: Nothing in the fridge

A couple scour the fridge for a few morsels and discover that they are richer than they thought.

Scene

Living room of a house; MAN and WOMAN arrive home. They slump down on the sofa, exhausted.

Woman:	*(Big sigh)* What a day.
Man:	Yeah, I'm absolutely whacked. Shall we just veg out this evening? Get a takeaway? Where's the menu for that Chinese place?
Woman:	Oh no, I've just remembered—we've got people over tonight!
Man:	For dinner?
Woman:	No, for breakfast.
Man:	Ha, ha. Do you want to check the fridge?
Woman:	No, I want you to check the fridge.

(MAN braces himself to get up, pulls himself up from the sofa, goes through to the kitchen and opens fridge door.)

Woman:	How's it looking?
Man:	Nothing.
Woman:	Nothing?
Man:	Nothing.
Woman:	What do you mean?

Man:	We've got nothing in the fridge. (*Pause*) Apart from milk.
Woman:	I thought we had some eggs.
Man:	Yes, three eggs. Bit of cheese. Pack of bacon.
Woman:	What about the leftover lasagne?
Man:	Still here. And an old sausage wrapped in tinfoil. Unless it's a bionic finger in cold storage.
Woman:	Any veg?
Man:	Just some tired-looking cabbage. Some sleepy broccoli. And a bit of soporific spinach.
Woman:	There must be some sauce in there?
Man:	No.
Woman:	Behind the jam and chocolate spread.
Man:	Oh yeah. Only Thai sweet chilli, mayonnaise, tomato and brown sauce. There's a pot of yoghurt.
Woman:	What flavour?
Man:	Rhubarb.
Woman:	Well, that hardly counts.
Man:	We're nearly out of parmesan. And the cream's out of date.
Woman:	I see what you mean. Nothing.
Man:	How old's that salmon?
Woman:	'Bout a week.
Man:	Better chuck it. Still, there should be half a packet of biscuits in the tin.
Woman:	We can't offer biscuits for dinner.

(*MAN returns to living room.*)

Reproduced with permission from *Drama out of a Crisis*, BRF 2012 (978 0 85746 005 9) **www.barnabasinchurches.org.uk**

Man:	Who's coming over anyway? Friends or…?
Woman:	Family.
Man:	*(Sits back on the sofa)* We had your mum and dad over last year.
Woman:	No, it's Mol and Tol and the kids.
Man:	That's a new one on me. Where did they spring from?
Woman:	Cambodia.
Man:	Thought all your relatives came from Croydon?
Woman:	I said they were family, not relations. Their pond's nearly empty and all their fish are dying.
Man:	Take them to the aquarium.
Woman:	The fish aren't decorative. It's all they've got to eat.
Man:	Well, we're hardly overloaded with supplies. Unless you want to open a tin of soup or some baked beans, we'll have to go to the 24-hour supermarket.
Woman:	We'll do that, then.
Man:	But it's a ten-minute drive. And I've just got comfy.
Woman:	Takeaway?
Man:	Did you find that leaflet?
Woman:	No.
Man:	We'll have to cancel. Phone them and say something's come up.
Woman:	But they're expecting dinner.
Man:	Invite them over another time.
Woman:	I'm not phoning. It's embarrassing.
Man:	Send them a text, then.

Woman:	But what are we going to eat?
Man:	Last night's lasagne? You send a message. I'll bung it in the microwave.
Woman:	We'll do a big shop tomorrow.
Man:	Get it delivered. It's only a fiver. Fancy a biscuit while we wait?

(WOMAN picks up her mobile.)

(Note: For a provocative and perhaps, for some audiences, uneasy ending, finish here. For an ending which 'ties up the loose ends' and suggests that sharing is the right answer, finish with the lines below.)

Woman:	No, I can't do it. I mean, if they've got nothing else…
Man:	And if they are family…
Woman:	Let's share with them what we have.

END

*

Malaria

No flies on me

Curtain up

Although it's a preventable and treatable disease, malaria is a huge public health problem today in more than 100 countries where 2400 million people live—that's 40 per cent of the world's population. Malaria is estimated to cause up to 500 million clinical cases and over one million deaths each year. Children, in particular, are vulnerable to malaria. In Africa, where 80 per cent of malaria cases are treated at home, the disease kills one child in 20 before the age of five.

Spread by mosquito bites, malaria transmission can be simply and easily reduced through the distribution of inexpensive mosquito nets and the use of insect repellents. The mosquito population can also be cut by basic control measures such as spraying insecticides inside homes and draining standing water where mosquitoes lay their eggs.

Bible backdrop

Jesus went to every town and village. He taught in their meeting places and preached the good news about God's kingdom. Jesus also healed every kind of disease and sickness. When he saw the crowds, he felt sorry for them. They were confused and helpless, like sheep without a shepherd.
MATTHEW 9:35–36

'Confused and helpless' is an apt description of the millions of people under threat from malaria across the globe. We read in Matthew that when Jesus saw disease and the way it affected people, he felt compassion and healed them. While there's a natural (rather than just a supernatural) answer to malaria, it is still miraculous. Mosquito nets cost less than £5, and every fiver is a lifesaver.

Sermon prompt

This sketch offers a straightforward introduction to the worldwide problem of malaria. With so simple a solution, we've got to ask why malaria hasn't already been tackled among the world's poorest people. The sad conclusion is that maybe there just isn't sufficient international 'will' to make it happen.

Do we see the lives of people who live in poverty as less valuable than ours? Is an African person's life so cheap that we'd prefer to fuel our own pursuit of material possessions than to save lives? It's a hard message for a sermon, but these are good questions to ask.

Taking it further: Learn the facts

Tearfund's International Learning Zone (TILZ) provides plenty of facts about the disease and ideas for preventing the spread of malaria. If your church is connected to projects in a malarial area, you could pass on some useful learning to them. Visit http:tilz. tearfund.org and search for 'malaria' to find resources in English, French, Spanish and Portuguese.

Cast

Two insects make up the cast, MOSQUITO 1 and MOSQUITO 2. They can be male or female. They could speak with a 'buzzy' tone to their voice, to emphasise their insectile nature.

Staging: props, costumes and effects

To make the characters seem more like mozzies, they can be dressed simply in black, move on tiptoe (enthusiastic stagers can add two false legs) and make swift, insect-like movements. They both need to clutch at straws (actually rather than metaphorically).

Script: No flies on me

Two blood-sucking mozzies discuss the deadly consequences of their feeding habits.

Scene

MOSQUITO 1 is seated, sucking happily on a long straw.
MOSQUITO 2 buzzes over to join MOSQUITO 1.

Mosquito 2. Is it? Is it? Can I say it? *(Mosquito 1 is still sucking)* 'I knew, one day, we'd get to the bottom of it!'

(Mosquito 2 laughs heartily.)

Mosquito 1: If you had waited until I'd finished my sip, I would have told you. Look up there. It's a neck, and further up is a head. This is a shoulder. Nowhere near the... rear end.

Mosquito 2: Oh well, maybe one day! Budge up, you're hogging the best bit.

Mosquito 1: There's plenty of plasma for the two of us.

Mosquito 2: You're such a snob. Call it what it is: blood. Red, viscous, delicious human blood. *(Slurps)* Yum, yum. *(More slurping)*

Mosquito 1: It's uncouth insects like you—with dreadful table manners—that give us mosquitoes a bad name.

Mosquito 2:   Are you serious? We've got a bad name because we attack people late at night while they are sleeping and drain blood out of them.

Mosquito 1:   Yes, there is that.

Mosquito 2:   Oh, and if that's not nasty enough, we then squirt saliva containing proteins and enzymes into the wound. This causes an allergic reaction, leaving people with a nasty red itchy swelling.

Mosquito 1:   You make it all sound so horrible. I like to think we give people a special friendly nip while they are snoozing, and leave them with a lovely satisfying itch to scratch.

Mosquito 2:   Don't kid yourself. We're the lowest of the low. Bottom of the food chain.

Mosquito 1:   But we're not, are we? We may look like teeny-tiny flies that you could splat with one swat. But we're really deadly, vicious creatures of the night. Grrr.

Mosquito 2:   You don't scare me.

Mosquito 1:   We scare humans, though. Those big hulking beasts who think they've mastered the earth. There they are, building huge cities, flying about in planes, watching *Dickinson's Real Deal*. They think they rule the world. But one quick nip from little old me and... splat. How the mighty fall. Do you know, up to 500 million people catch malaria every year?

Mosquito 2:   *(Unimpressed)* Yeah, yeah, yeah.

Mosquito 1:   And the only way to catch it is through us. Forget tigers, tarantulas, sharks and piranhas.

We are, officially, the deadliest creature known to mankind. We kill more than one million people every year.

Mosquito 2: Well done, you. What if I told you that 90 per cent of those killed are the poorest people on earth? And the vast majority of them are children?

Mosquito 1: Just shut up and drink. Don't see you becoming a vegetarian.

Mosquito 2: I just don't know why you're so pleased with yourself. That's all. It's our fault.

Mosquito 1: It's easy to blame us. Blame the mosquito.

Mosquito 2: Yes it is. 'Cos it's us that causes it!

Mosquito 1: We're just doing what we do. We don't know better.

Mosquito 2: So whose fault is it, then?

Mosquito 1: Humans.

Mosquito 2: I knew you'd say that. Just an excuse for you to keep sucking blood without having to worry. *(Sarcastic)* Of course it's the humans' fault. They're the ones who lie there with their flesh exposed. It's like they want to be bitten and die.

Mosquito 1: But it's not like they can't prevent it. Alongside all the drugs that are available, a treated mosquito net only costs £5. Just a fiver to save a life but there's still millions of cases every year.

Mosquito 2: OK. You've convinced me. It's a diet of fruit and vegetable juice from now on.

Mosquito 1: Really?

Mosquito 2: Really. You going to join me?

Mosquito 1: I'm not sure I'm ready. But I'll give it a go if you do…

Mosquito 2: You're giving up?

Mosquito 1: Yes.

Mosquito 2: Great. Plenty more blood for me!

Mosquito 1: I thought you said you were quitting.

Mosquito 2: Don't know if anyone's ever told you this. My friend, sometimes you're a real sucker. Let's drink!

END

*

Living with HIV

Masterblind

Curtain up

It's currently estimated that across the world nearly 33 million people are living with HIV, a disease that devastates communities. This huge loss of life, with illness on such a scale, has significantly affected the ability of governments and other organisations to cope. In some highly affected countries, it has reversed progress on development, and in entire communities the pandemic is intensifying poverty, with children often suffering the most. Local churches have a huge role to play in offering relief and support to affected communities and influencing government decisions about access to treatment.

Bible backdrop

The Lord forgives our sins, heals us when we are sick.
PSALM 103:3

Despite the stigma and prejudice attached to the name, HIV is a virus like any other, and something that God is determined to heal. However, many people in the UK and across the world are still guilty of the sin of unfairly maligning and disregarding people living with HIV.

Sermon prompt

In the 1980s, the UK government raised awareness of HIV and AIDS with this catchy slogan: 'Don't die of ignorance'. Unfortunately, many of the misconceptions and wild inaccuracies about HIV still persist, and other urban myths have sprung up, not only in this country but also in countries where HIV is prevalent. One of the key ways to tackle any problem is to understand it fully and use that knowledge to begin to do something about it.

People living with HIV, or those who have AIDS, are often described as 'modern-day lepers' because of the fear and misunderstanding provoked (and let's not forget, leprosy is still a huge problem, too). We see from Jesus' encounters with people who had leprosy that he knew enough about the disease to recognise that he could have normal human contact with them without becoming infected. He didn't see anything in their plight to suggest that people who suffer from leprosy should be treated any differently. They could still be healed and restored and could receive salvation the same as anyone else.

Since the 1980s, when HIV and AIDS were raised to our collective radar, much has happened and there have been significant breakthroughs in the treatment and prevention of HIV. It would be great if more people knew and understood these developments. Then HIV would be considered less like a huge uncontainable problem, and more like a significant issue for which steps can be taken to overcome it.

Taking it further: Learn more about HIV

In the spirit of the above and the moral of the sketch, it would be good to encourage your church (through small groups or other networks) to learn more about HIV and AIDS. There are many resources available on the internet that give a true picture of the facts. You might like to start by browsing the Tearfund International Learning Zone website: http:tilz.tearfund.org. Simply search for HIV and you'll find technical policy reports and guides.

Cast

Just two parts: HOST and CONTESTANT. They can be male or female.

Staging: props, costumes and effects

Both performers should be in smart and formal dress, and should maintain that air of formality in their performance. The set is simple: a chair and desk for the HOST and a swivel chair for the CONTESTANT. In keeping with the programme, you should have some atmospheric lighting (if available), such as a spotlight on the CONTESTANT. If you can, play the Mastermind music and sound effects in the appropriate places.

Script: Masterblind

A know-all gets quizzed on his HIV expertise and finds that ignorance isn't bliss.

Scene

Just like the TV show, Mastermind, a besuited presenter (HOST) is seated at a desk opposite a swivel chair, which is in spotlight.

Host: May I have our first contender, please?

(Enter CONTESTANT, who sits, looking nervous)

Host: Your name?
Contestant: Noel Bighead.
Host: Occupation?
Contestant: Armchair Philosopher and general Smart Aleck.
Host: Your chosen specialist subject?
Contestant: Human immunodeficiency virus or HIV.
Host: Noel Bighead, you have two minutes on human immunodeficiency virus or HIV starting... now. What happens if you are infected with HIV?
Contestant: You die.
Host: Incorrect. Of course everyone will eventually die but, with correct treatment, many people with HIV can still live a long healthy life. True or false: you can catch HIV from a mosquito bite?
Contestant: True.

Reproduced with permission from *Drama out of a Crisis*, BRF 2012 (978 0 85746 005 9) www.barnabasinchurches.org.uk

Host:	Incorrect. There is no scientific evidence to support this claim. What is the best way of treating HIV?
Contestant:	There isn't one.
Host:	Incorrect. It's antiretroviral treatment, which keeps the amount of HIV in the body at a low level and stops any weakening of the immune system. HIV infection rates are most prevalent in which group?
Contestant:	Homosexuals.
Host:	Incorrect. It's estimated that 80 per cent of HIV infection is through heterosexual intercourse. How would you describe HIV testing?
Contestant:	Unreliable.
Host:	Incorrect. Modern HIV testing is around 99 per cent accurate. If a woman has HIV, what will happen if she has a baby?
Contestant:	The baby will be HIV positive too.
Host:	Incorrect. There is around a 25 per cent risk, but with early treatment it can be just 2 per cent. What is the difference between HIV and AIDS?
Contestant:	Nothing.
Host:	Incorrect. HIV is a virus and AIDS is a collection of illnesses. True or false, HIV is a curse from God?
Contestant:	Um. (Thinks) Pass.
Host:	If you don't have any symptoms, does that mean you don't have HIV?
Contestant:	Yes.

Host:	Incorrect. HIV infection can take more than ten years to become a full-blown virus. Name four ways of becoming infected with HIV?
Contestant:	Toilet seats, kissing, tattoos and hugging.
Host:	Incorrect. Only one of those can, in very rare cases, infect you with HIV.
Contestant:	Which one?
Host:	Incorrect. I'm asking the questions. What is the— *(Buzzer sounds)* I've started so I'll finish: What is the biggest lesson you've learnt today about HIV?
Contestant:	That I don't really know very much about HIV. And I really need to learn more—and soon.
Host:	Correct! And at the end of that round, Noel Bighead, you have only scored one point—but it's a good one! You passed on one: True or false, HIV is a curse from God? Well, if it is, then so are all viruses. HIV is just another viral infection like tuberculosis, pneumonia and the flu. Just like those, it can be caught by anyone, and it's a killer. So maybe HIV should be everyone's specialist subject. Goodnight.

END

Reproduced with permission from *Drama out of a Crisis*, BRF 2012 (978 0 85746 005 9) **www.barnabasinchurches.org.uk**

*

Global sanitation crisis

Big jobs

Curtain up

People often find it embarrassing to talk about toilets, but this reluctance to be open about sanitation is part of the reason why an estimated 2.6 billion people worldwide are without proper loos. The result is that poor communities often lack protection against preventable diseases that kill thousands of people daily, particularly children.

Half of the young girls who drop out of school in Africa do so because they have to trek huge distances to collect water for their families, or because there are no toilets at their school. Often, girls are left open to attack or sexual assault (which can lead to HIV transmission) because they have to travel far to find a hidden spot to go to the toilet—away from the safety of home. Consider this: in the minute that has just passed, three children under the age of five have died because of unclean water and unsafe sanitation, and another three will die in the next minute...

Bible backdrop

Set up a place outside the camp to be used as a toilet area... You must keep your camp clean of filthy and disgusting things.
DEUTERONOMY 23:12, 14A

In contrast to our taboo, God doesn't have a problem talking about toilets. In Deuteronomy 23, God sets out his plan for a clean camp.

It's as important as instruction on worship, religious festivals, war and marriage. It's also seen as a spiritual issue: if a camp is clean, God is more at home dwelling there.

Sermon prompt

This sketch offers a fun way to introduce the subject of sanitation and the global toilet crisis. Many in the congregation may be surprised to learn about the detail that the book of Deuteronomy goes into when discussing the disposal of human excrement.

If you need extra inspiration, there are some great short films at www.tearfund.org/makelifeflow, plus ideas for sermons, small groups, prayer and worship. The films and resources tell the story of 13-year-old Stidia, who lives in Kigazi village in Uganda. Every day she used to make two trips down a steep, dangerous mountain to fetch water from a spring. But Stidia's life and community have been transformed, thanks to Tearfund's church partners and their mission to make access to clean water and decent sanitation a reality.

Taking it further: Kick up a stink

Why not set off a stink bomb at church? They're easily available from joke shops or online. What would your congregation think if they arrived at church to be faced with a nasty smell? How uncomfortable would they feel? Would they be able to worship?

Once you've let off the bomb, ask people how it made them feel. Then point out that the smell is the least of the problem. Human excrement carries deadly diseases such as cholera, and lack of sanitation can cause severe diarrhoea—which kills more children than AIDS, malaria and measles combined.

Cast

There are three parts in this sketch: PRIEST 1, PRIEST 2 and PRIEST 3. All should act like enthusiastic students and can be of any gender but, if you want to be historically accurate, they should all be male.

Staging: props, costumes and effects

Each of the three priests needs a scroll to open, and they should all be dressed in long flowing robes (a quick way to get this effect is to cut a head-sized hole in a big blanket or length of material).

Script: Big jobs

Three priests get the jobs of a lifetime, and one gets a lifetime of jobs.

Scene

PRIEST 1, PRIEST 2 and PRIEST 3 all rush in, clutching scrolls sealed with a ribbon.

Priest 1:   What you got? What you got?

(Grabs at 2's scroll, who resists)

Priest 2:   Excuse me! *My* scroll, I'll open it. What's in yours?

(Makes a grab; 1 pulls his scroll away and hides it behind his back)

Priest 3:   That was magnificent. I think we priests really learnt something today. What a sermon!

Priest 1:   Yes, it was really... long.

Priest 2:   Quite incredibly... lengthy.

Priest 3:   Brilliant, though. Old Moses covered a lot of bases.

Priest 1:   Obeying God, worshipping in one place, not worshipping other gods...

Priest 2:   What food is clean, what's not, cancelling debts, how to treat servants...

Priest 3:   Firstborn animals, Passover, Feast of Weeks, Feast of Tabernacles...

Priest 1:   Judges, law courts, the king...

Priest 2:   Giving offerings to priests and Levites!

Priest 3:   Loved that bit! (*Others agree*)

Priest 1:   Bring it on!

Priest 2:   I must confess, I did nod off a bit in the middle.

Priest 3:   'Resting in the Lord', I think it's called.

Priest 1:   With added dribbling.

Priest 2:   It was a very, very deep contemplation. Did I miss much?

Priest 1:   There sure was a *lot* of stuff in there.

Priest 3:   It certainly wasn't three points all starting with the letter 'J'.

Priest 1:   Or an acronym. I love a good acronym-based sermon. I once did one about parenting teenagers that made up the acronym EXASPERATING. The E stood for 'Emotional trauma'; X was for... 'Xylophone', for some reason...

Priest 2:   But we're forgetting something. The scrolls!

Priest 3:   The scrolls!

Priest 1:   The scrolls! (*Beat*) What's in yours?

Priest 2:   Let's see yours first.

Priest 3:   Stop squabbling. We'll open them together. After three. (*Beat*) One...

Priest 1:   Oh, I'm so excited!

Priest 3:   Two...

Priest 2:   Me too. I can't wait to see what I've got!

Priest 3:   Three!

Reproduced with permission from *Drama out of a Crisis*, BRF 2012 (978 0 85746 005 9) www.barnabasinchurches.org.uk

(They unroll the scrolls together, tentatively. Each examines the contents)

Priest 1:   *(Waving a triumphant fist)* Result!

Priest 2:   *(Looks overwhelmed; falls to his knees)* I am truly blessed.

(PRIEST 1 and 2 look to 3. He stares, exasperated, at his scroll. They move behind him to see what he's got. PRIEST 3 rolls up his scroll hurriedly so as not to show them)

Priest 3:   *(Underwhelmed)* Good. Great, in fact. Yes. Fine.

Priest 1:   Something the matter?

Priest 3:   *(In denial)* No. No. No.

Priest 1:   *(To 3)* What did you get?

Priest 2:   *(Butting in)* I have been awarded the section about war and conflict. Just to think, I shall now spend my whole life studying and interpreting the laws covering battles and disputes with other nations. What higher calling can there be?

Priest 3:   Well done. That is, as you say, very impressive.

Priest 1:   Huh. War, violence and destruction? I wouldn't sully my studies with it. On the other hand, I have been selected to disseminate the intricacies of the laws about offerings to priests and Levites. Such an honour. *(Rubbing his hands)* Lucrative too, I shouldn't wonder.

Priest 2:   Well done, I'm sure. *(To 3)* And what did you get?

Priest 3:   Yes. I got something equally... interesting. *(Changing the subject)* So there we are. We all have our subjects of priestly study.

Priest 1:   But what did you get?

Reproduced with permission from *Drama out of a Crisis*, BRF 2012 (978 0 85746 005 9) **www.barnabasinchurches.org.uk**

Priest 3:   What did I get? (*Hides scroll behind his back. PRIEST 2 sneaks behind to see*) It's a very, um, crucial aspect of everyday… life. (*PRIEST 2 grabs the scroll*)

Priest 2:   Got it!

Priest 1:   (*Crowding round*) Let's have a look… Oh. (*Disgusted*) Urgh.

Priest 2:   Yuck.

Priest 1:   (*Reading*) 'Uncleanness in the camp.'

Priest 2:   (*Reading*) '… if something happens at night that makes a man unclean and unfit for worship, he must go outside the camp and stay there…'

Priest 3:   As I said, vital laws and practical guidance…

Priest 1:   (*Reading*) '… set up a place outside the camp to be used as a toilet area…'

Priest 2:   (*Reading*) '… and make sure that you have a small shovel in your equipment…'

Priest 1:   (*Reading*) '… when you go out to the toilet area, use the shovel to dig a hole…'

Priest 2:   (*Reading*) '… then, after you relieve yourself, bury the waste in the hole…'

Priest 3:   (*Repeating*) '… in the hole.' Yes. There are a lot of, er, nuances there. Plenty of deep, hidden meanings that I'll have to draw out of the text.

Priest 1:   It's about… doing a (*sotto voce*) number two, isn't it?

Priest 3:   Ostensibly, yes—if you take the words in their literal meaning. I mean, there must be many and various ways of approaching the passage.

Priest 2:   There's a euphemism for you. (*PRIESTS 1 and 2 crack up with laughter*)

Priest 3:	Yes, yes, you can laugh.
Priest 1:	We are. *(Cracks up again)*
Priest 3:	I suppose you think you're so important just because you got laws about war and priestly offerings.
Priest 1:	*(Serious)* No, you're right, yours is just as important. In fact, it's a very big job! *(They both laugh again)*
Priest 3:	*(Defiant)* Actually, it is. It's important. Vital, in fact. Essential.
Priest 2:	Don't kid yourself. You got the crappy part— literally.
Priest 3:	*(Convincing himself)* A clean camp... is a healthy camp. God knows what he's talking about, you know. If people left their... you know what... everywhere, we'd be in a right state. If there's no way to clean up after yourself, then people get diseases. *(Convinced)* And you can't fight in a war or give offering to a priest if you are ill... or if you die from a disease. People can't work... can't look after their families... can't worship God. Not in an unclean camp. How about that?
Priest 1:	Good point.
Priest 2:	Quite.
Priest 3:	So you'd better hope that I'm good at passing on these laws. For all our sakes. Eh?
Priest 1:	We're very sorry.
Priest 2:	Yes, you're right, we were wrong to pooh-pooh them! *(Cracks up)* Sorry, couldn't help myself.

END

Reproduced with permission from *Drama out of a Crisis*, BRF 2012 (978 0 85746 005 9) **www.barnabasinchurches.org.uk**

*

Water crisis

Water cooler moment

Curtain up

During the 20th century, the world's population tripled, but we
now use more than six times the volume of water that we did just
a hundred years ago.

Current estimates suggest that the world's population will
increase by another 50 per cent in the next 50 years. Add this to
industrialisation, urbanisation and climate change, and demand for
water will be huge—with catastrophic consequences for human
health and the environment.

That's why the world's supply of fresh water is running out and,
already, one person in five has no access to safe drinking water.

Bible backdrop

Generosity will be rewarded: give a cup of water, and you will
receive a cup of water in return.
PROVERBS 11:25

For all its 'pie in the sky' reputation, the Bible is very down to
earth about most subjects. This proverb recognises that generosity
doesn't just benefit the receiver. With H_2O growing scarcer,
something very alarming is looming: wars over water. Yes, the most
abundant liquid on this planet will soon be in such short supply
that people will take up arms to acquire it. So let's be generous:

let's treat water as something precious and supply water to parched populations—for their sake and ours.

Sermon prompt

It would be great to examine how precious a commodity water was shown to be in the Bible, particularly in the Old Testament, using examples such as the pool of Beersheba (Genesis 21:19), Isaac's well (24:11), Jacob's well (John 4:6), the Pool of Siloam (9:7) and the waters of Nephtoah (Joshua 15:9). You could also examine the spiritual symbolism of water (for example, in baptism) and Jesus' use of the phrase 'living (or life-giving) water' (John 7:38).

Next, give examples of how little we value water—allowing taps to leak, sprinkling lawns and running huge baths. In fact, the only time we seem to value water is when it's bottled and sold to us, even though our taps offer the same commodity for free.

Now look for examples of how water is valued in countries where there are no taps, where people walk miles to find a well.

Taking it further: Water challenge

Alarming statistics reveal that the average European uses 200 litres of water every day, while the average person in the developing world lives with only ten. In order to experience what that's like, Tearfund's youth team have devised a Water Challenge: can you live on just ten litres of water a day?

This fun and thought-provoking challenge helps young people and adults get to grips with the subject and can be used to raise awareness in your church, too. To find details, enter 'Tearfund water challenge' into your search engine of choice.

Cast

There are two cast members: WORKER 1 and WORKER 2. They can be male or female.

Staging: props, costumes and effects

The main thing you'll need for this sketch is some kind of giant water dispenser, such as a garden water butt, and a laptop (I suggest using an old one or mocking one up, in case of water damage). You'll need to allow for quite a bit of water spillage, so it might be good to perform the sketch at an outdoor event (or have a team of people ready with mops at the end). Oh, and keep away from wires, plugs and anything electric!

Script: Water cooler moment

Two thirsty office workers take some much-needed time out.

Scene

A huge office water cooler is centre stage. WORKER 1, dressed in a bedraggled business suit, crawls on to the stage—breathless, hot, thirsty and soaked in sweat and dust. WORKER 1 feebly holds a small plastic cup to the water cooler tap. Gulping down the cool, refreshing water, WORKER 1 repeats this several times, pouring and swallowing drink after drink. Shortly after, WORKER 2 arrives in a similarly bedraggled state, falling down in front of the water cooler. WORKER 1 notices WORKER 2's collapsed state and pours a cup of water.

Worker 1:   Here you go, get this down you…

(WORKER 1 helps WORKER 2 to drink)

Worker 2:   *(Gasping)* Six miles.
Worker 1:   Bit of a trek, eh?
Worker 2:   Didn't think I'd make it. The heat…
Worker 1:   It is a bit on the warm side of scorching. Still, you're here now. Drink up.
Worker 2:   Thank you. *(Gulps down another cup, with water running down face)*
Worker 1:   Did you get those quarterly figures over to Jay in Finance?

Reproduced with permission from *Drama out of a Crisis*, BRF 2012 (978 0 85746 005 9) **www.barnabasinchurches.org.uk**

Worker 2:   No, we still need to offset the VAT. *(Drinks again)* Plus I was a little thirsty, you know?

Worker 1:   *(Drinks)* Yes.

Worker 2:   Got the rough figures on my laptop. Here.

Worker 1:   *(Goes to turn on laptop)* Oh, you seem to be out of battery.

Worker 2:   Plug it in.

Worker 1:   We're in the desert.

Worker 2:   Oh yeah. Just have to wait till we get back.

Worker 1:   Did you see *The Apprentice* last night?

Worker 2:   Yes, what a bunch of idiots. *(Beat)* Can you grab me another cup of water?

Worker 1:   *(Obliging)* Here you go. *(WORKER 2 drinks)* Got to leave you to it, I'm afraid. I'm presenting an advertising pitch at 3pm. It's going to take me half an hour to get back…

Worker 2:   What are you pitching?

Worker 1:   It's a new irrigation system. Flowing water straight to the workplace. A revolutionary new concept in H_2O delivery.

Worker 2:   Well, good luck with that. *(Drinks again)*

Worker 1:   Can't see them buying it. One for the road. *(Drinks up and leaves. WORKER 2 collapses)*

END

Reproduced with permission from *Drama out of a Crisis*, BRF 2012 (978 0 85746 005 9) www.barnabasinchurches.org.uk

*

Education and poverty

School's out

Curtain up

Across the world, more than 100 million don't go to school or have any access to it. The vast majority of children who are denied education live in poor countries, and around two-thirds are girls. Lack of education and skills leaves children and young people with fewer opportunities and choices, a legacy that locks whole populations into long-term poverty.

Bible backdrop

Teach your children right from wrong, and when they are grown they will still do right.
PROVERBS 22:6

The Bible teaches that education is an amazing thing, but it is far more transformative than we might imagine. Good education can reduce poverty, improve health, prevent HIV and give people the freedom to be good citizens in their communities and nations.

Sermon prompt

In 2011, I visited western Nepal, where a form of slavery called 'bonded labour' had been widespread until ten years previously.

Talking to the people who were kept as slaves, I found that it wasn't just financial constraints that kept them in bondage; it was also absence of education. One of the things they most valued—that the church had provided for them—was a primary school for their children. They knew it was education that would ultimately provide them with real freedom.

This sketch addresses one way in which children are denied education, and, while the cause seems unusual, it is extraordinarily widespread. Lack of adequate water and sanitation facilities is a major factor in preventing children from attending and thriving at school. The sketch clearly addresses the factors that cause this lack.

It would be great to broaden this idea to include how we receive teaching from God and from church. Where would we be if we didn't have guidance? How could we cope if we were prevented from receiving biblical teaching?

Taking it further: Soul Action

The message about the importance of education might come as a surprise to some of the school-age people in your church—particularly the teenagers, who may not want to be at school at all. We in the developed world, who have benefited from universal education for so long, often do not value schooling enough, but we'd definitely miss it if it was denied to us.

It's essential to educate young people about poverty and justice —to raise important world issues that they may never encounter otherwise. Soul Action is a joint initiative between Tearfund and Soul Survivor, which aims to inform young people about poverty and encourage them to get involved in prayer, campaigns and action. Visit www.soulaction.org to find out more.

Cast

There are only two cast members, PUPIL and TEACHER, who could be male or female. If TEACHER is female, PUPIL should use the alternative dialogue 'Miss, Miss!' rather than 'Sir, Sir!' (this is indicated in the script).

Staging: props, costumes and effects

If you can, set out a few school desks; if not, improvise with tables. The main signifier should be the costumes, and it would be good to go for extremes: TEACHER in a cape and mortar board, PUPIL in traditional school uniform (such as blazer, shirt and stripy tie).

Script: School's out

A teacher begins to understand the surprising reasons why his class size is diminishing.

Scene

A school classroom. All desks are empty apart from one. TEACHER enters, oblivious to the lack of pupils.

Teacher:	*(Sits at his desk, not looking)* Good morning, class.
Pupil:	*(Cheeky)* All right, chief?
Teacher:	*(Unpacking briefcase, looks cross)* Listen here, class 2P. I know we've been forced to make some *(looks up, notices there's only one pupil)* cutbacks… but that doesn't mean we don't treat today like every other day.
Pupil:	*(Puts hand up)* Sir! Sir! [Miss! Miss!]
Teacher:	Let me finish. When I enter the room, I say, 'Good morning, class', and you respond…?
Pupil:	Good morning, Mr [Miss] Point.
Teacher:	Thank you.
Pupil:	*(Puts hand up)* Sir! Sir! [Miss! Miss!]
Teacher:	Kindly reserve your question until I've taken the register. *(Opens register)* Now, Class 2P, I will read out your surnames in alphabetical order. Let's start: Adams. Adams. *(Pause, looks up)* Adams?
Pupil:	He's ill.

Reproduced with permission from *Drama out of a Crisis*, BRF 2012 (978 0 85746 005 9) www.barnabasinchurches.org.uk

Teacher:	I can't just write 'ill'. What's he ill with?
Pupil:	Diarrhoea.
Teacher:	Thank you. That's d... i... a... r... um. No, it's d... i... a... y? Um, d... y...? I'll just put 'tummy bug'. *(Pupil puts hand up)* At the end, please. *(Back to register)* Where were we? Bell? Bell? *(Pause, louder)* Bell?
Pupil:	Can't be the bell, sir, we've only just started.
Teacher:	Pay attention, 2P! Is Sally Bell present?
Pupil:	No. She's got diarr... a tummy bug too.
Teacher:	Cooper?
Pupil:	Tummy bug.
Teacher:	Davis?
Pupil:	Tummy bug.
Teacher:	Evans?
Pupil:	Ditto.
Teacher:	*(Pours himself a glass of imaginary water)* Must be something going around.
Pupil:	Same with Fox, Goodman, Hamilton and Irving.
Teacher:	Oh dear. I wonder what caused it? *(Gulps from the glass)*
Pupil:	They drank the water.

(TEACHER spits imaginary water all over the floor)

Pupil:	Thanks, sir.
Teacher:	Don't answer back. *(Back to register)* Jolley? Jolley? *(Pause)* Jolley?
Pupil:	Not now you've spat dirty water all over the place.

Reproduced with permission from *Drama out of a Crisis*, BRF 2012 (978 0 85746 005 9) www.barnabasinchurches.org.uk

Teacher:	Calm down, Class 2P. Is Jack Jolley absent?
Pupil:	He's gone with Jill King to fetch some water.
Teacher:	That's no excuse. *(PUPIL puts up hand)* Questions at the end, please. *(PUPIL puts hand down)*
Pupil:	Thanks to your cutbacks, the nearest water supply is now two miles away.
Teacher:	Class 2P, that's ridiculous!
Pupil:	So they'll be a bit late in, as will Lang, Mear, Nicholson and Oliver.
Teacher:	But we only cut back on non-essential services.
Pupil:	Like toilets and fresh water?
Teacher:	We are in the business of education: pens, paper and calculators are our water. And learning, achieving and league tables are our...
Pupil:	Toilets?
Teacher:	*(Continuing)* What about... Potts? Potts? *(Pause)* Potts?
Pupil:	We can't use them, it's unsanitary.
Teacher:	Pay attention, 2P. Where is Emily Potts? Has she come down with this tummy bug, or is she away fetching water?
Pupil:	Bitten, sir.
Teacher:	Bitten? By what?
Pupil:	A snake.
Teacher:	You what?
Pupil:	Now the loos have gone, we have to go in the nature area—where the school snake lives.
Teacher:	That's not a good enough reason, 2P.
Pupil:	When you've got to pee, you've got to pee.

Teacher:	What about *(Reads off list)* Roberts, Smith, Thomas, Upton, Vincent, Williams, Xavier, Young and Zappa. What's their excuse?
Pupil:	Water, tummy bug, water, water, snake, tummy bug, water…
Teacher:	And Zappa?
Pupil:	Present, sir.
Teacher:	A tick at last. Good. *(PUPIL puts hand up)* Now, Zappa, what's this question you've been burning to ask all morning?
Pupil:	Um, can I be excused, sir?

END

Reproduced with permission from *Drama out of a Crisis*, BRF 2012 (978 0 85746 005 9) www.barnabasinchurches.org.uk

*

Children at risk

What if?

Curtain up

Across the world, millions of children are caught up in conflict or grinding poverty, traumatised by war, homeless, hungry, starved of love and exposed to sexual abuse or exploitative labour.

There are around one billion children living in poverty—that's half the children in the world. Of those, 640 million live without adequate shelter, 400 million have no access to safe water and 270 million have no access to health services.

Childhood poverty is a long-term problem, as opportunities lost while growing up are not easily regained later. When children experience poverty, even for a short time, it can affect them for the rest of their lives. For example, malnutrition in early childhood can lead to lifelong learning difficulties and poor adult health.

Bible backdrop

Some people brought their children to Jesus so that he could bless them by placing his hands on them. But his disciples told the people to stop bothering him. When Jesus saw this, he became angry and said, 'Let the children come to me! Don't try to stop them. People who are like these little children belong to the kingdom of God.'

MARK 10:13–14

Here we see Jesus' compassion for the children of the world. Jesus doesn't just see them as unformed adults, but offers children as a picture of the kingdom of God. How great a contrast it is that these infants, who are so precious to God, are often so badly overlooked or mistreated in the world today!

The passage at the end of the sketch is taken from Lamentations 2:19 (NIV).

Sermon prompt

Given the billions of children living in poverty, this sketch offers a way to make those figures tangible—even amusing. The audience's laughter at the seemingly absurd statistics should change to shock as they realise that these figures relate to children.

It would be good to follow this with a talk about how we can judge the state of the world by the suffering of those who are most vulnerable. It would also be good to emphasise the opportunity offered by childhood to instil good values and to provide safety and freedom, so that children can prosper and thrive. You could point out the opportunity we all have to do what we can—through prayer, giving and campaigning—to offer a better start to suffering children across the world.

Taking it further: Join Viva

Viva is a network of organisations (including Tearfund) that aims to give more children a safer, happier and brighter future. Viva's vision is for a comprehensive, collaborative and transformational Christian response to the needs of children at risk worldwide, allowing children and those working with them the opportunity to be all that God intends.

If you'd like to get involved and support Viva's work, visit www. viva.org. You can join in prayer, become a volunteer or become a church partner.

Cast

There are four 'voices', ONE, TWO, THREE and FOUR, all of whom can be played by someone of any age or gender.

Staging: props, costumes and effects

This is an opportunity to be creative in staging. You might like to consider scattering the performers (or readers) throughout the church congregation. Alternatively, the sketch could be performed in semi-darkness or candlelight.

Script: What if?

Voices cry out for children devastated by poverty.

Scene

ONE, TWO, THREE and FOUR all arrange themselves on stage.

One: What if everyone in Newcastle was a slave?

Two: Or if every British plumber was forced to fight in brutal wars?

Three: Perhaps if all of Sky TV's UK customers died of preventable diseases?

Four: Or if every person who has ever been on an Alpha course was sold as a sex slave?

One: What if all Liverpudlians died of measles?

Two: Or if everyone in a UK home with internet access was an AIDS orphan?

Three: Perhaps if everyone who went on a Hoseasons holiday died from diarrhoea?

Four: Or if everyone in Britain who owns a Ford Focus died from drinking dirty water?

One: What if everyone in the UK who wears contact lenses was HIV-positive?

Two: Or if everyone who's a member of a British gym died because they weren't immunised?

Three: Perhaps if everyone who has seen the musical *Grease* died before their fifth birthday?

Reproduced with permission from *Drama out of a Crisis*, BRF 2012 (978 0 85746 005 9) **www.barnabasinchurches.org.uk**

Four:	Or if every self-employed person in the UK died in their first month of life?
One:	What if everyone in Britain who plays a musical instrument died of malnutrition?
Two:	Or if everyone in the UK who owns a caravan died through lack of vitamin A and zinc?
Three:	Perhaps if the entire population of the British Isles had never been to school?
Four:	Or if everyone in Europe was without adequate shelter?
One:	What if all the Facebook users in the world didn't have a clean water supply?
Two:	Or if everyone across the globe who plays football was denied medical treatment?
Three:	Perhaps if all those Geordies, plumbers, Sky TV subscribers...
Four:	Alpha course attendees, Scousers, internet surfers...
One:	Hoseasons holidaymakers, Ford Focus drivers, contact lens wearers...
Two:	Gym bodies, Grease lightnings, self-employed workers...
Three:	Musicians, caravanners, British citizens...
Four:	Europeans, Facebook pokers and footballers...
One:	Were children?
Two:	Living in slavery, fighting in wars, dying of curable diseases...
Three:	Sold as sex slaves, succumbing to measles, orphaned by AIDS...

Reproduced with permission from *Drama out of a Crisis*, BRF 2012 (978 0 85746 005 9) www.barnabasinchurches.org.uk

Four:	Dead from diarrhoea, killed by dirty water, HIV-positive…
One:	Perished not immunised, gone before aged five, or in the first month of life…
Two:	Starved to death, lost through lack of vitamins, uneducated…
Three:	Without a home, no clean water and never seen a doctor?
Four:	Arise, cry out in the night, as the watches of the night begin…
One:	pour out your heart like water in the presence of the Lord.
Two:	Lift up your hands to him for the lives of your children…
Three:	who faint from hunger…
Four:	at every street corner.

END

Reproduced with permission from *Drama out of a Crisis*, BRF 2012 (978 0 85746 005 9) www.barnabasinchurches.org.uk

*

Maternal health

From here to maternity

Curtain up

'Maternal health' is a phrase describing the health of mothers when they are pregnant and during childbirth and the weeks shortly after. While, for many, being a mum is an amazing life experience, for others it can mean pain, severe health problems and even death.

Some of the main causes of death in mothers include infection, haemorrhage, high blood pressure, unsafe abortion and obstructed labour. According to the World Health Organisation:

- Every day, approximately 1000 women die from preventable causes related to pregnancy and childbirth.
- 99 per cent of all maternal deaths occur in developing countries.
- Maternal mortality is higher in rural areas and among poorer and less educated communities.
- Adolescents face a higher risk of complications and death as a result of pregnancy than older women.
- Skilled care before, during and after childbirth can save the lives of women and newborn babies.
- Between 1990 and 2008, maternal mortality worldwide dropped by one-third.

Bible backdrop

Children are a blessing and a gift from the Lord.
PSALM 127:3

Given the alarming statistics above, the psalmist's declaration here is far removed from the experience of millions of women across the world. I'm not saying that the scripture is wrong, more that we must extend the blessings that we in the developing world enjoy to mothers across the world.

Sermon prompt

It's amazing how many times pregnancy and parenthood are described in the Bible as being a blessing from God (for example, Genesis 21:2; 25:21, 1 Samuel 1, and Luke 1:26–45). However, the Bible doesn't shy away from the fact that in times of hardship, it is pregnant women and young mums who particularly suffer (Luke 21:23).

Through the Holy Spirit, scripture urges us to have compassion and to take action on behalf of those who are vulnerable and weak. Young mums and mums-to-be should be high on our list.

Taking it further: Micah Challenge

Tearfund campaigns as part of Micah Challenge, a movement of people and organisations around the world who aim to take up Old Testament prophet Micah's challenge to oppose the injustice of poverty. Micah Challenge proposes that the Millennium Development Goals offer the best opportunity the world has ever had to eliminate extreme poverty, and is bringing the church together worldwide in a united cry for this opportunity to be realised.

The fifth Millennium Development Goal is to improve maternal health. The targets are to reduce by three-quarters the maternal mortality ratio and achieve universal access to reproductive health. If you want to be part of Micah Challenge and help to halve world poverty, visit www.micahchallenge.org.

Cast

This is a dramatic monologue (in verse), so there's only one cast member, MOTHER, who is female. Learning lines is always best but, if time is tight, the script can be openly read. It is essential to practise the piece so as to capture the shift in tone at the end.

Staging: props, costumes and effects

None needed.

Script: From here to maternity

A mum-to-be chooses only the best for her baby, and realises how privileged she is.

Scene

MOTHER enters the stage.

Mother: I'm saying goodbye to mouldy old cheese
So long, Stilton, Roquefort and all types of Bries

Throw out marlin, shark and spiky swordfish
Don't want heavy mercury near my dish

But please load me up with oily poisson
I want the slipperiest of fish to feast upon
Lob salmon, mackerel, and pilchard at me
So tasty, light and rich in Omega-3

With all those little fishes, baby will be fine
In the development of the brain and spine

I'm also skipping coffee and cups of tea
For nine whole months, no caffeine for me
And alcohol too, don't get me started
Wine, gin and Prosecco all sadly departed

When you rustle up an omelette, just as a safeguard,
Cook those eggs until they're absolutely rock hard

And if my head is splitting, I won't say it again,
Please don't tempt me with ibuprofen
I'll keep my headaches under control
With a moderate dose of paracetamol

Stub out all fags, don't puff on cigars
And stay away from smoke-filled cars

And if my heart burns with acid indigestion
Naughty antacids are simply out of the question
If the pain won't subside, and I feel a desperate need
I'll use a heartburn remedy derived from seaweed

Yes, I'm throwing my fake tan straight in the bin
In case dihydroxyacetone should penetrate the skin

You can't be too careful in this day and age
I want baby to be perfect in every way
And whether little junior is a he or a she
I won't put this new life in jeopardy

So when the waters break, rush me straight to the
clinic
That has all those wonderful machines within it
And if endorphins alone won't make the pain pass
Load me up with nitrous oxide gas
Give me pethidine, opioids and sweet fentanyl
Don't hold back, doc, I'm taking them all

Reproduced with permission from *Drama out of a Crisis*, BRF 2012 (978 0 85746 005 9) **www.barnabasinchurches.org.uk**

I want baby to be born in a sterile, clean place
Not with germs and infection littering the place
A midwife to hand, a husband to squeeze
And sling in an epidural as well, if you please

I'm sorry, you what?
I can't believe what you say
A thousand mums still die every day?
From complications in pregnancy and preventable disease?
And 99 per cent in developing countries?

(Pause)

So, when they place my baby
In my arms,
For the very
First time

And I see the little
Twinkle
In his eyes

I'll remember,
In my heart,
All those millions of mums
Who'll never live to see
Their daughters or sons

END

Reproduced with permission from *Drama out of a Crisis*, BRF 2012 (978 0 85746 005 9) www.barnabasinchurches.org.uk

*

Ending violence against women

Deadlier than the male

Curtain up

'Globally, women between the age of 15 and 44 are more likely to be maimed or die as a result of male violence than through cancer, malaria, traffic accidents or war combined.' *(United Nations Secretary-General's in-depth study on violence against women, 2006)*

Take a pause, then read that again. Yes, being a woman is the deadliest killer on earth. Violence against women is the world's most common but least punished crime, and it's worse if you live in poor or corrupt countries where there's little chance of conviction.

Bible backdrop

But Amnon would not listen to what she said. He was stronger than she was, so he overpowered her and raped her.
2 SAMUEL 13:14

The story of Amnon in 2 Samuel is a shocking example of the violent abuse of male power. In contrast to this, in John 8:3–11 we see Jesus' compassionate, gentle treatment of a 'sinful' woman brought to him by the Pharisees to be judged. Like Jesus, we must make a stand and challenge violence and abuse of women at all levels, from casual sexism among friends or colleagues (and in the church) to large-scale abuse of women—for example, in conflict situations where rape and sexual violence are used as weapons of terror.

Sermon prompt

Despite the deeply disturbing subject matter, this sketch is essentially a light-hearted comedy (albeit with extremely sinister undertones). Because of this contrast, it would be a good sketch to perform before a talk that introduces issues of gender violence, looking at biblical and practical examples of how this outrage should be dealt with.

A great source of information and resources about violence against women can be found on the Restored website: www. restoredrelationships.org. Here you'll find Q&As, statistics, films and resources for churches. Restored is a global Christian alliance that aims to transform relationships and end violence against women. An alliance that developed out of Tearfund's work, Restored believe that Christian churches have huge potential to help prevent violence, but that they also need to change their own attitudes and practice.

It is worth considering the pastoral consequences of raising such issues. Domestic abuse of women is so prevalent that it is very likely that some members of your congregation may have been abused (or are still being abused). Make sure you have considered ways for those affected to receive help and support, such as contacting a local or national counselling service or advice centre.

Taking it further: Challenge abuse

Sadly, women are still maligned and seen as 'fair game' for abuse at work and in social situations. Are you prepared to stand up and challenge people who are casually abusive towards women in their words and actions? We should adopt a zero-tolerance approach to the abuse of women.

Cast

Two performers: DOCTOR is male and EILEEN is female.

Staging: props, costumes and effects

You'll need á desk, a couple of chairs and some papers but little else.

Script: Deadlier than the male

A woman visits her doctor after tests, and is shocked by some surprising results.

Scene

A doctor's surgery. DOCTOR JOLLEY is sitting behind a desk, reading through some papers. There is a knock at the door.

Doctor: Come in. Ready or not.

(Enter EILEEN, tentatively)

Eileen: Hello. *(Unsure)* Doctor…?
Doctor: No. No. No. Not me. I'm just the chap who cleans out the tropical fish tank.
Eileen: I have an appointment with Doctor Jolley?
Doctor: That's me! Jolley by name… *(Looks glum)* Sadly, not by nature. *(EILEEN is silent)* That's a joke.
Eileen: Oh. I'm here to pick up the results of my tests?
Doctor: One minute! Just got to finish reading these… *(Reads papers)* Hmm. Yes. Oh dear… Dear, oh dear. Nasty… very nasty.
Eileen: *(Concerned)* Something wrong?
Doctor: You could say that. My wife has been sneakily voting for that young boy with the doey eyes.
Eileen: I don't understand?

Reproduced with permission from *Drama out of a Crisis*, BRF 2012 (978 0 85746 005 9) www.barnabasinchurches.org.uk

Doctor: The X-Factor. Got the phone bill here. I'm sure we agreed to back the blonde girl with the nice feet. I wondered why my wife spent such a long time in the loo on Saturday. And she did sneak the phone in with her…

Eileen: My tests?

Doctor: Oh, yes, the results. Let's have a look. (*Examines*) Good. Yes, all seems well, nothing to worry about. (*EILEEN sighs*) Congratulations, Steve, it's all cleared up. (*Offers his hand to shake, looks her up and down*) You're not Steve! (*Beat*) Are you?

Eileen: No.

Doctor: You must excuse me, bit of a mix-up with the results. So, who are you, then? And what's wrong with you?

Eileen: Eileen.

Doctor: Left or right?

Eileen: Sorry?

Doctor: Which way do you lean?

Eileen: No. My name's Eileen. And I thought *you* were going to tell *me* what's wrong.

Doctor: Eileen… Eileen. (*Rifles through his papers*) Yes, here we are. (*Solemn*) Oh. Gosh. My heavens. (*Beat*) I think you'd best sit down, Eileen.

Eileen: I'm… already seated.

Doctor: Better get up, then. (*EILEEN rises to her feet, tentatively*) Now you'd better sit down.

Eileen: (*She sits down again*) If there's something wrong… I'd prefer if you just told me straight out.

Doctor:	I'm afraid it's very serious. These results are deeply worrying.
Eileen:	Is it... *(Swallows)* is it terminal?
Doctor:	Oh, no, no, no. *(Beat)* I'm afraid it's much worse than that.
Eileen:	Worse than... Doctor, please tell me what it is.
Doctor:	I'm afraid these results are irrefutable proof that you are... a woman.
Eileen:	I'm a... woman. Is that serious?
Doctor:	Deadly.
Eileen:	Oh.
Doctor:	Across the world, women your age are more likely to be maimed or die from violence than through cancer, malaria, traffic accidents or war. Combined.
Eileen:	Violence? What sort of violence?
Doctor:	At least one in every three women has been beaten, coerced into sex or otherwise abused in her lifetime.
Eileen:	But who's doing this?
Doctor:	Men.
Eileen:	But that's... that's terrible.
Doctor:	It doesn't stop there, I'm afraid. Domestic violence is the largest form of abuse of women. And the number of women forced or sold into prostitution worldwide could be up to four million.
Eileen:	Is there anything I can do?
Doctor:	There are certain precautions you could take...
Eileen:	Such as?

Doctor:	Don't be poor. Don't be young. Don't get old. Don't have a disability or an illness. Don't get married. Don't have children. But, above all, stay away from men!
Eileen:	But why should I have to live my life like that? It's not my fault. Why don't you stand up and do something about this?
Doctor:	Me? What should I do about it? It's really not my problem.
Eileen:	Yes it is!
Doctor:	No, it's not. It's got nothing whatsoever to do with me. I don't need to worry about it, because —thank goodness—I'm a man.

END

*

Natural disasters

Massive earthquake

Curtain up

More than 90 per cent of people killed or affected by natural disasters are in poor communities. The appalling devastation caused by the 2010 earthquake in Haiti offers a clear example of how vulnerable poor countries and communities are to sudden shifts in their natural environment.

While it's not clear whether seismic activity is increasing (the trend shows an increase but that may be because of more and better recording equipment), what is certain is that media reporting of natural disasters is escalating. That's a really good thing but it does mean that TV viewers are becoming more used to seeing devastation on a massive scale, which means that we may become desensitised to it.

Bible backdrop

Don't get tired of helping others. You will be rewarded when the time is right, if you don't give up.
GALATIANS 6:9

When faced with huge and seemingly relentless and insurmount-able global problems such as natural disasters, it's easy just to give up or get cynical. The Bible talks a great deal about the value of perseverance: we should keep praying and offering what help we can, however many times we are called upon to do so.

Sermon prompt

When Jesus used the example of wise and foolish builders in Matthew 7:24–27, he was highlighting the need to make good choices and be prepared. For many years, Tearfund, among other aid agencies, has pioneered 'disaster risk reduction'—a way of helping poor communities who are vulnerable to natural disasters to prepare and make wise choices about their environment.

However, reducing risk can only go so far. We must also be prepared so that agencies such as Tearfund can respond as soon as disasters strike. The first 48 hours are the most vital when providing aid after a natural disaster. Tearfund has a disaster fund so that there are resources ready and available for an emergency response immediately after a crisis. One great way of reducing the impact of a disaster is to give regularly to Tearfund's disaster fund rather than responding when a disaster happens. Sadly, if you see a disaster on the television, for many of those affected it may already be too late.

Taking it further: Keep up the good work

If you've given to an appeal after a natural disaster, why not check up to see how your donation has been spent? Visit the website and look for updates or request an Annual Report. Also, when you read stories of survivors and rebuilding projects, pray for them. You may find that you are prompted to keep on giving.

Cast

There are only two people in the cast: ONE and TWO. They could be housemates or a couple, so any gender mix is possible.

Staging: props, costumes and effects

The set-up is very simple: a sofa or a couple of comfy chairs in front of a TV (with a remote control) are all that is needed. Put the back of the TV stage front, with the back of the set facing the audience, so that the two performers can stare at the telly and still be seen by the audience.

Script: Massive earthquake

Two friends watch a massive disaster unfold on TV, and find it quite engrossing.

Scene

ONE is sitting passively, the TV remote in hand.

One: Oh, I can't watch. *(Covers eyes)*

(TWO enters, picks up TV guide)

Two: Anything on telly tonight?
One: This is quite exciting.
Two: What is it?
One: It's a new thing on News 24.
Two: What's it called?
One: 'Massive Earthquake'.
Two: It's a repeat.
One: Don't think so.
Two: Yeah, this was on a few months ago.
One: No, that was 'Devastating Floods'. This is a new series. That was set in Asia. This is the Caribbean, or somewhere.
Two: Have I missed much?
One: It's day eight now. But the story's easy to pick up.
Two: What's happened so far?

One: It's one of those 'high concept' things. It started with a teaser trailer. Just a message saying that a massive earthquake has hit and there would be 'more to come'.

Two: Why does everything have to be so hyped up these days?

One: Then the programme started a few hours later and, I must say, it was all a bit depressing. The main character seems to be this gruff news reporter type.

Two: 'With relationship issues...' no doubt.

One: And, for what seemed like hours, all he did was chase ambulances and scour hospitals looking for all these dead and injured people.

Two: Did they show the moment that the earthquake hit?

One: Only in flashbacks. It was all very arty—footage from mobile phones and CCTV. But you did see lots of cars and stuff get crushed. Buildings collapsing.

Two: Wicked.

One: That didn't last long and it was on to the injured. But once you've seen one wailing survivor... They do the X-Factor trick of giving them all heartbreaking backstories. One girl had a Polaroid of her dad... lost in the earthquake. Another was crying over her baby... lost in the earthquake. Someone else couldn't find her cat...

Both: (In unison) ... lost in the earthquake. (Pause)

Two:	Is that the gruff news reporter...?
One:	That's him. He's following this search and rescue team, digging people up out of the rubble.
Two:	Sounds tedious.
One:	It's quite tense, actually. They do all this build-up. A dog sniffs something up, or they find life signs. All thermal imaging cameras. Then they dig about to try to find someone trapped. Always the same pattern.
Two:	Bit predictable, then.
One:	The aftershocks liven things up. They all stop and run away, shouting at the camera about how every second is vital. But it was amazing yesterday—they found this one little girl who'd been trapped under the rubble for seven days.
Two:	That's stretching credulity. Sometimes they treat us viewers like idiots.
One:	Idiots, yeah. But when they pulled her up... I don't mind saying, I cried. I actually cried.
Two:	You're so susceptible.
One:	You didn't see it. It was amazingly well done.
Two:	What's that phone number keeps flashing up at the bottom?
One:	Some kind of interactive thing. You phone the number, or press the red button, and pledge some dosh.
Two:	Flipping cheek!
One:	I might phone and offer a tenner.
Two:	They've got to you, then.

One: I've really enjoyed it so far. And I'd quite like them to keep going, do another series. *(Picks up the phone, dials and waits as it rings)*

Two: It's just boring. Wait a minute, look at those looters scrambling about for scraps of food. You go grab it, mate. Ha ha! Now the army are waving guns at them. What you gonna do now, mate? Hit him with your stick? He's got body armour on, you twit.

One: *(On phone)* Hello, is that Massive Earthquake? Yes, I'd like to pledge some money. *(Listens)* £10.

Two: Hey, give them a fiver from me. This is starting to get interesting...

END

Reproduced with permission from *Drama out of a Crisis*, BRF 2012 (978 0 85746 005 9) www.barnabasinchurches.org.uk

*

Climate change

Bridge over troubled water

Curtain up

While there is still some debate about the details of climate change, among the world's most eminent scientists there is a significant consensus that the world is getting warmer, and that human beings have played a significant part in causing that warming.

Tearfund, among other aid agencies, works on climate change because extreme weather patterns hit the poorest people hardest. Poor communities across the world tell Tearfund that they are already feeling the impact of changes to their environment. Unpredictable rainfall means more droughts and floods. More droughts mean a greater risk of famine; more floods mean greater destruction of homes and livelihoods and the potential for infectious diseases to race through the population.

Bible backdrop

The earth and everything on it belong to the Lord. The world and its people belong to him.

PSALM 24:1

The Bible challenges us to love the people around us, but our selfish consumption of unclean energy is already causing death and devastation to poor communities across the world. We must speak out and protect God's creation and the precious people who live on the earth, by calling on governments to reduce greenhouse gas emissions and offer financial assistance to help poor countries adapt to the destructive impact of climate change.

Sermon prompt

Climate change. Of all the global threats which face our planet, this is the most serious.
JOHN STOTT, *THE RADICAL DISCIPLE* (IVP, 2010)

It seems quite inexplicable to me that there are some Christians who claim to love and worship God, to be disciples of Jesus, and yet have no concern for the earth that bears his stamp of ownership. They do not care about the abuse of the earth, and indeed, by their wasteful and over-consumptive lifestyles, they collude in it.
CHRIS WRIGHT, *THE MISSION OF GOD* (IVP, 2008)

Matthew 22:34–40 explains that the pinnacle of a good and holy life is the perfect love that exists between each of us and God, and with our neighbours. The root of evil is when these relationships are broken, with God or with others. Our failure to love God means that we don't care about the things God cares about, including the earth and all the people whose lives depend on the earth. Although we all depend on the earth's resources to survive, currently climate change poses the most imminent threat to those in greatest need.

The Jubilee Centre and Tearfund have produced a set of five Bible studies by Nick Spencer and Robert White, designed to examine the Christian approach to climate change and sustainable living. The studies are free to download from Jubilee Centre's website, www.jubilee-centre.org (search Resources/Bible Studies). These would be a great starting point for a sermon or small group study.

Taking it further: Carbon Fast

You can help combat climate change, and demonstrate to the people around you that you care about God's creation, by taking part in Tearfund's annual Carbon Fast during Lent. The fast offers simple actions and prayers to help people reduce their carbon footprint and protect poor communities from the changing climate. To take part, visit www.tearfund.org/carbonfast.

Cast

This is a dramatic monologue, so there's only one cast member, MAYOR, who could be male or female. Learning lines is always best but, if time is tight, the script can be read openly, as it is supposed to be a speech.

Staging: props, costumes and effects

Not much staging is required (MAYOR could simply stand at a lectern) but it would be good to give the character a few mayoral costume signifiers, such as a chain, robes or even a hat.

Script: Bridge over troubled water

Mayor's speech at the opening of a damaged bridge, which no one is prepared to cross.

Scene

MAYOR enters and stands behind the lectern.

Mayor: Welcome, everyone, to the grand opening of our new bridge. Before I declare the bridge open, I'd like to thank you for your patience. It's been 14 years, three months and ten days since the bridge was first completed. As you no doubt remember, the opening ceremony was interrupted by a loud cracking and rumbling sound, followed by falling masonry—and then by people frantically fleeing for their lives.

Many still believe that this should have been the end of the bridge, which the local press have dubbed 'death-trap crossing'. People weren't satisfied when we downgraded the bridge from being suitable for heavy traffic to taking only small motor vehicles with their engines removed. No one was prepared even to cycle over it, or to walk across slowly and purposefully, holding the hand-rails. Even when it was declared fit for

Reproduced with permission from *Drama out of a Crisis*, BRF 2012 (978 0 85746 005 9) www.barnabasinchurches.org.uk

small rodents, not a single child offered their pet hamster to test it.

Many have scoffed at our attempts to fix the bridge, saying that applying two layers of domestic paint was simply not sufficient to rectify the major structural shortcomings of the design and build. But we decided not to listen to the dissenters or to be put off by the alarming headlines in the local press. No, what we needed was a solid professional opinion. So we asked a qualified structural engineer to test the bridge. It took him just 14.3 seconds to proclaim it a write-off. We sent him back, demanding a full scientific assessment, but, sadly, further tests revealed that the bridge was in a far worse state than he at first thought.

Rather than seeing this as a setback, we simply sought a second opinion from another eminent engineer, who offered an equally scathing opinion on what he called 'an utter disgrace of a structure'. But we were determined not to let the clear scientific assessments that we'd received prevent us from believing that the bridge was, in fact, pretty OK really—if not great to look at, with all the steel supports sticking out at strange jaunty angles.

So we asked more engineers, architects and other qualified persons to examine the bridge.

Reproduced with permission from *Drama out of a Crisis*, BRF 2012 (978 0 85746 005 9) www.barnabasinchurches.org.uk

And—unsurprisingly, some said—each one found more and more alarming reasons why it should not be used under any circumstances. But we know that our community needs a bridge! As people venture out each morning in little dinghies or wetsuits, or simply stripped down to their undies, we know that we need something to carry us safely and drily over the river. We need it because our jobs, our relatives and even the public toilets are on the other side of the bank. We simply need a crossing!

Some people have said we should just pay whatever it takes to repair it. They say it makes economic sense to shell out. But I can now tell you that we don't need to spend any money or make repairs!

Yes, nothing needs to be done, because at last we have found someone to examine the bridge who can give us the result we want to hear! Yes, after 99 structural engineers trotted out the same old mantra that it's unfit to be walked on, or that a gentle gust of wind might blow it over, we have found someone—our 100th expert—who says that the bridge is, and I quote, 'Perfectly fine'. And that 'It's a lot of fuss over nothing.' Sadly, he can't be with us today because he was rushed to hospital owing to a stray breeze-block that ricocheted off his head shortly after he gave the bridge the all-clear.

Unfortunately, there has been a messy and unnecessary smear campaign against our expert. But, just because he hasn't got the 'right qualifications' or the 'professional expertise' to give an opinion, that doesn't mean he shouldn't have his say! And you've got to ask yourself the question, are you going to listen to the opinions of 99 qualified structural engineers or the simple assessment of a man who, by his own admission, 'doesn't really know much about bridges'? Today, we have a choice: we can either accept the final judgment or the 99 previous opinions. I think we all know the right answer…

So, if I could ask you all to line up… One by one we will cross the bridge and put an end to this nonsense once and for all. And, as a mark of my humility, I'm prepared to be the very last person to cross the bridge. *(Pause)* Who would like to volunteer to go first?

END

Reproduced with permission from *Drama out of a Crisis*, BRF 2012 (978 0 85746 005 9) www.barnabasinchurches.org.uk

*

Climate change

Environmentally challenged...

Curtain up

On average, a UK home produces six tonnes of heat-trapping carbon each year. Up to a third of that can be saved by taking small steps and becoming more energy-efficient. You don't have to attach a wind turbine to your roof just yet (unless you want to!) but you could start by turning electrical equipment off standby.

If we all took everyday steps to reduce carbon emissions, it would save us money, keep the earth cool and help protect poor communities from climate change.

Bible backdrop

No one who loves others will harm them. So love is all that the Law demands.
ROMANS 13:10

In this verse, the apostle Paul describes perfect love—something that does no harm to others. As part of our walk with Jesus, we must do our best not to harm our neighbours (who include all people across the world) by playing our part to reduce climate change-causing emissions.

Sermon prompt

'Going green' has a lot of bad press: it's portrayed in adverts and newspapers as confusing, difficult and a nuisance. The reality is that there are simple ecological solutions to most problems. Also, using sustainable products is getting easier as environmentally friendly items become more widely available. We learn from the Bible that God hates waste—not just wasted lives but wasted resources, too. He values people who work hard and find the best (not always the easiest) solutions, and he encourages people to plan ahead (see Matthew 7:24–27). The truth is that we need to find a way of living that builds not on the sand of fossil fuels but, rather, on the rock of renewables.

Taking it further: Become a greener church

If we want to convince governments and business that we are serious about climate change, we must first take steps ourselves. Tearfund has produced a booklet, *Play Your Part*, which will help your church get to grips with environmental issues. Then you can collectively investigate ways to reduce waste at your church through reducing, reusing and recycling. Remember, this should be a fun as well as a challenging journey.

Cast

There are three cast members, PRESENTER, JO and CHRIS, who have been cunningly named so that they can be played by people of either gender. Choose different names if you wish.

Staging: props, costumes and effects

The set should be simple. PRESENTER needs a microphone, and JO a green paint pot and brush (available in DIY shops). They could wear printed T-shirts, which would be fun but not absolutely essential.

Script: Environmentally challenged...

Have fun with St Able and St Upid as they challenge climate change.

Scene

PRESENTER, a smart TV host, enters.

Presenter: Welcome to Church Climate Change Challenge Live! Today we're meeting two churches that have been transformed to reduce their contribution to climate change. Welcome Chris from St Able's and Jo from St Upid's!

(Enter CHRIS, wearing a T-shirt with the slogan 'We are St Able!', and JO, wearing a T-shirt with the slogan 'We are St Upid!' JO is holding a paintbrush and paint pot.)

Presenter: Let's start with you, Chris. How has St Able changed to be more energy-efficient?

Chris: *(Joking)* Well, let's state the obvious first. Becoming a 'greener' church doesn't mean painting your church green!

Jo: Doesn't it? *(Throws brush and paint pot off stage)* Um, of course it doesn't.

Presenter: So, what did you do, Chris?

Chris: First we looked at what the Bible says and examined the scientific evidence. We wanted the church to understand that climate change is already happening—and it's hitting poorest people hardest.

Presenter: Jo, did you do something similar at St Upid?

Jo: As always, we did things our own St Upid way. We put a notice up with the health and safety regulations: 'Like it or lump it, we're going green.'

Presenter: I see. Chris, how has St Able reduced its carbon footprint?

Chris: We now use mugs instead of disposable cups.

Jo: At St Upid we only boil a kettle with enough water for one cup at a time. So if you want tea at the end, you have to queue for two and a half hours.

Presenter: You're supposed to boil only enough for what you need, not one at a time. Didn't you read the guidelines?

Jo: Sorry, we recycled them. I thought that's what you wanted.

Presenter: Um, back to Chris. How else have you inspired the church to be more energy-efficient?

Chris: We ran a series of sermons about how love does no harm to its neighbour, to help us grasp that what we consume has an effect on poor communities across the world.

Jo: So did we. First week, the sermon was 'What would Jesus drive?' We got drivers of 4x4s to

Reproduced with permission from *Drama out of a Crisis*, BRF 2012 (978 0 85746 005 9) **www.barnabasinchurches.org.uk**

stand up while we booed them. We followed it up with 'Turn your thermostat down or burn (in the eternal fires of human-induced climate change)'.

Presenter: That's, um, interesting. Chris, how has St Able risen to this church climate change challenge?

Chris: It's definitely a journey. Sometimes it was a question of trying to find out the right thing to do. Should you wash nappies at high temperatures or use disposables?

Jo: Dunno about you, Chris, but I've stopped wearing them altogether.

Presenter: *(Ignoring Jo)* But you have made a difference at St Able?

Chris: Oh, yes. People now cycle, walk or give each other lifts to church. And we have significantly reduced our climate change-causing emissions.

Jo: Significantly reduced? At St Upid, we've reduced our emissions 100 per cent!

Presenter: Incredible! How did you manage that?

Jo: Everyone's left the church.

Presenter: It seems that St Able have put the 'logical' in ecological, whereas St Upid have put the 'mental' in environmental. And I know which church I'd rather belong to. Goodbye!

END

Reproduced with permission from *Drama out of a Crisis*, BRF 2012 (978 0 85746 005 9) www.barnabasinchurches.org.uk

*

Trade justice

Nothing but the tooth

Curtain up

Trade justice is crucial to helping people out of extreme poverty, but current trade rules and practices overwhelmingly favour developed nations, and wealth and power are increasingly found in the control of a small number of international players. It's incredible to consider that some individuals and businesses control more wealth than whole countries.

International trade is a massive business, yet many of the goods we purchase in the UK have been manufactured in countries where workers receive very low wages and often work in appalling conditions.

Bible backdrop

'I, the Lord, love justice.'
ISAIAH 61:8

Justice is central to the very nature of God. There is no place in God's kingdom for oppression, poverty, exploitation and injustice. So it's a spiritual battle to try to take on and challenge these things.

Sermon prompt

The Bible introduces us to a God who is our refuge, who cares for those who are poor and needy. The Lord's desire is to protect the weak, and he calls on his people to do the same. Yet unjust trade rules make it almost impossible for poor workers and producers to get a fair price for their goods and enjoy the rewards of their hard work.

The Lord's Prayer encourages us to thank God every day for his provision but, for many people, the riches that the world provides (and we benefit from) are stolen from others. We must be aware and uncomfortable that many poor workers and producers around the world are denied trade justice. Their lives are intrinsically linked to ours, because they are like us—made in God's image—and they are connected to us through global trade.

Injustice in global trade lies at the heart of the inequality in our world today. Trade rules are a key factor in deciding who is rich and poor and whether our environment is protected or spoilt. They affect people's lives, livelihoods and habitats, and they are often grossly unfair.

Taking it further: Hold a Created gifts fair

Tearfund supports craft workers and artisans from poor communities across the world, encouraging them to develop and market high-quality products. A Tearfund initiative, Created (formerly known as Tearcraft), sells beautiful and useful gifts, handcrafted by skilled artisans across the world. When you buy from Created, you can be certain that the workers have good employment, have received a fair price and can expect a better future.

So why not set up a stall and sell some Created gifts at your church? When people get to see and feel the products, it makes all the difference in demonstrating that these really are beautiful, well-crafted items. To help this happen, Created makes display kits of products available to registered sellers.

You could also encourage someone from church to become a Created seller and join the team of volunteers who, in return for a small discount, sell goods on Created's behalf. To find out more and make contact, visit www.createdgifts.org.

Cast

There are just two characters in the cast: CONSULTANT and FAIRY. While CONSULTANT can clearly be male or female, you don't necessarily have to have a female playing FAIRY. In fact, a great deal of fun could be had from having a big burly man in a tutu playing the fairy.

Staging: props, costumes and effects

The staging is simple: two chairs and a desk. CONSULTANT should have a notepad and papers and so on. He or she should look office-smart and have an officious air. As noted above, FAIRY should be instantly recognisable as a fairy—a pink tutu, tights, wings and matching magic wand.

Script: Nothing but the tooth

The tooth fairy seeks career guidance but finds that there's no magic wand to end injustice.

Scene

FAIRY enters and sits down opposite CONSULTANT.

Consultant:	How can I help you?
Fairy:	I need some career guidance.
Consultant:	*(Aside)* And some fashion tips, by the looks of it. *(Looks up)* Career guidance! You've come to the right place. I'm sure we can set you on the right path. First I need a few details. What's your surname?
Fairy:	Fairy.
Consultant:	Oh. And your first name?
Fairy:	The.
Consultant:	So, your name is 'The Fairy'. That's a little… out of the ordinary.
Fairy:	I usually use my middle name.
Consultant:	Which is?
Fairy:	Tooth.
Consultant:	Oh, I see, so it's…
Fairy:	The Tooth Fairy.
Consultant:	Well, The Tooth Fairy, how can I help you?
Fairy:	I'd like some advice about my employment. Things aren't quite as lucrative as they used to be.

Reproduced with permission from *Drama out of a Crisis*, BRF 2012 (978 0 85746 005 9) **www.barnabasinchurches.org.uk**

Consultant:	I'd have thought being The Tooth Fairy was a job for life. Children will always shed teeth!
Fairy:	Yes, but nowadays I can't seem to make ends meet.
Consultant:	Let's get to the... er... root of the problem. Don't you just collect a tooth from under a pillow and leave some small change?
Fairy:	Yes, but I used to get a good return for the discarded gnashers I'd collect. If, by the end of the week, I had a couple of incisors, a few canines and a handful of molars, I'd be smiling.
Consultant:	What went wrong? Do you feel you're not getting your bite of the cherry?
Fairy:	Not any more.
Consultant:	What changed?
Fairy:	Brace yourself for a long story. First thing you've got to understand is that I'm not the only Tooth Fairy. There's loads of us all over Fairyland. There has to be—the amount of teeth we collect.
Consultant:	I see. And you all do the same job?
Fairy:	Yes. But we don't all get the same treatment. I come from a poorer part of Fairyland, and the rich fairies ganged up and fixed it so that they get most of the profit. There was a time when I could just about feed and educate my family from my earnings. But now... well, it's like pulling teeth.
Consultant:	Can you explain how bad it is?

Reproduced with permission from *Drama out of a Crisis,* BRF 2012 (978 0 85746 005 9) www.barnabasinchurches.org.uk

Fairy: Where I come from, we get less than half a per cent of the price of teeth worldwide. And that's less than half of the amount I got 30 years ago.

Consultant: Can't you just demand better prices?

Fairy: Things are stacked against us. In the rich places, the fairies are subsidised so that they can sell teeth for less. They're encouraged to gather far more teeth than they can possibly sell. So they dump the excess teeth on us. With the market flooded, the teeth I collect are worth even less.

Consultant: Why don't you just sell your teeth in these rich places?

Fairy: I'd love to, but there are all these rules and tariffs that prevent us from doing that. If I try to sell to rich places, my prices are too high because of these charges.

Consultant: Sounds like you need to demand better conditions.

Fairy: The problem is that, being a poor fairy, I don't have the same labour rights as the rich fairies. Many of the fairies I know don't work for themselves, collecting teeth from pillows. They've taken jobs in big tooth factories where they face a terrible daily grind. Conditions are awful, wages are rock-bottom and you're treated like dirt.

Consultant: And this is happening to poor fairies across the world, you say...

Fairy: All over. I'd love to keep at it but it's just not worth it. What can I do?

Reproduced with permission from *Drama out of a Crisis*, BRF 2012 (978 0 85746 005 9) www.barnabasinchurches.org.uk

Consultant:	Doesn't sound like there's much you can do. You'll have to just, um, grit your teeth and get on with it.
Fairy:	So you can't help me?
Consultant:	I'll tell you what, leave your CV with me, and I'll see what I can do.
Fairy:	Thank you very much. Goodbye.
Consultant:	Goodbye. *(FAIRY leaves, CONSULTANT picks up phone)* Send in the next. How did the last one go? Waste of time. Tried to string me along with some old fairy story. Unbelievable.

END

*

Fair trade

Shopping and fudging

Curtain up

When you buy fairly traded goods, you know that workers in developing countries are getting fair prices and enjoy good working conditions and that you are investing in local sustainable produce.

The Fairtrade Foundation website, www.fairtrade.org.uk, says:

The Fairtrade Foundation is the independent non-profit organisation that licenses use of the FAIRTRADE Mark on products in the UK in accordance with internationally agreed Fairtrade standards.

Our vision is of a world in which justice and sustainable development are at the heart of trade structures and practices so that everyone, through their work, can maintain a decent and dignified livelihood and develop their full potential.

To achieve this vision, Fairtrade seeks to transform trading structures and practices in favour of the poor and disadvantaged.

The Foundation requires companies to pay sustainable prices that must not be less than the market price. By doing this, they address the injustices of conventional trade, which often discriminates against the poorest, least powerful producers. That helps those producers to improve their standing, giving them more choice over their lives.

Bible backdrop

You refused to pay the people who worked in your fields, and now
their unpaid wages are shouting out against you. The Lord All-
Powerful has surely heard the cries of the workers who harvested
your crops.
JAMES 5:4

We've become used to cheap food, clothes and other goods. In
some ways, it would be easier not to know where our shopping
comes from, or why it's so cheap, but these unfair practices are not
hidden from God. He hears the cries of poor farmers and factory
workers. As his body on earth, we, the church, should be revealing
these chronic injustices and demanding that people are paid a fair
wage.

Sermon prompt

Why not start your talk by asking people to check the labels on
their clothes and to shout out where they have been made and
manufactured? That way, you can introduce the idea that we are
directly connected to poor workers across the world. Next, use
biblical examples to show why unfair practices are abhorrent to
God. There are plenty of good facts and statistics at www.fairtrade.
org.uk. Visit the 'Ideas for worship' section (Home > Get Involved
> Campaigns > Fairtrade Places > Fairtrade Churches > Ideas for
worship). Here you can find resources for reflection and study on
the theme of Fairtrade.

Taking it further: Become a Fairtrade church

You could encourage your church to become a Fairtrade church
and commit to using Fairtrade products, including tea, coffee,

sugar and biscuits. According to the Foundation, there are three goals to becoming a Fairtrade church. Your Church Council must agree to:

- Use Fairtrade tea and coffee after services and in all meetings for which you have responsibility.
- Move forward on using other Fairtrade products such as sugar, biscuits and fruit.
- Promote Fairtrade during Fairtrade Fortnight and during the year through events, worship and other activities whenever possible.

There are full instructions on how to become a Fairtrade church on the Fairtrade Foundation website: www.fairtrade.org.uk.

Cast

There are only two parts, STUDENT and ATTENDANT, which can be male or female. You might like to get someone who is of student age to play STUDENT.

Staging: props, costumes and effects

If you can, set up a few shelves with shopping on them to look authentic. Also, it's pretty essential to have a shopping trolley borrowed from a local supermarket, but make sure you return it afterwards.

For the costumes, the ATTENDANT should look as if he or she is in supermarket work clothes, and STUDENT should wear an exaggerated version of student attire. (Ask a student if you are not sure what this entails!) STUDENT will need a mobile phone.

Script: Shopping and fudging

A student's first trip to the supermarket ends in a trolley full of disappointment.

Scene

STUDENT is wandering up and down the aisle of a big hypermarket. ATTENDANT is stacking shelves, observing STUDENT curiously.

Student: *(On phone)* Hello, Mum. I just left Tins and Packets and took a right turn past Condiments and Table Sauces. I'm looking at a sign that says *(reads)* 'Toddler Toiletries'. Is this the right place to get *(consults list)* Krispy Kreme doughnuts? *(Listens)* Of course they're essential. I'm sure they count towards your five-a-day. How do I find where they are? *(Listens)* Yes, I know this is supposed to be my first solo shop, but I'm drowning in here…

(ATTENDANT comes over)

Attendant: Can I help you?
Student: *(On phone, whispers)* Some strange person has come over and started speaking to me. What should I do? *(Listens)* How are they dressed? They've got some sort of uniform on… and a badge. It says 'Ask me about our fantastic range

Reproduced with permission from *Drama out of a Crisis*, BRF 2012 (978 0 85746 005 9) www.barnabasinchurches.org.uk

of pork pies'. Should I do that? *(Listens)* Oh, that's good. I'll talk to them. Over and out.

Attendant: Hello.

Student: Hello, Friendly Supermarket Attendant.

Attendant: You look a little... in need of assistance.

Student: Yes. I'm doing a dry run.

Attendant: Oh. Pasta, rice and cereals are third aisle on the left, past Milk, Custards and Desserts.

Student: You see, this is the problem. A surprising number of the words and phrases that you've just used don't really mean anything to me.

Attendant: First time?

Student: My mum gave me this map but it's not really helping.

Attendant: Ah. There's a reason. This is a map of Tesco's. Tesco is over the road.

Student: Is that serious?

Attendant: You'll probably just have to navigate around without a map. Don't worry, I'll point you in the right direction.

Student: Phew. Now, I've made a few purchases already. I've bought a flat-screen TV, six T-shirts and two pairs of jeans, plus some CDs, DVDs and a car air freshener. It's shaped like a little tree. Smells like pine, apparently.

Attendant: What type of a 'shop' are you attempting to do?

Student: Oh, um. *(Looks at list)* It's called a 'food shop'. I'm practising for when I go to university.

Attendant: You've probably reached the stage now where you want to purchase some 'consumable items'.

Reproduced with permission from *Drama out of a Crisis*, BRF 2012 (978 0 85746 005 9) www.barnabasinchurches.org.uk

Student: Let me write that down. *(Writing)* After an hour and a half, it's time to purchase consumable items. *(Finishes)* Great.

Attendant: First you need to stock up on some staples.

Students: Staples. Great. So I'll find them in Stationery Refills and Accessories?

Attendant: No, no. I mean staple items. Things you'll always need to keep a good stock of.

Student: Like Häagen-Dazs, Hobnobs, Haribo and popcorn?

Attendant: I was thinking more of bread, milk, flour, sugar, coffee and tea.

Student: Tea! Yes. One of my plans at uni is to come home after a gruelling two hours of lectures and enjoy a *(consults list)* 'nice cup of tea'. So presumably, to do that, I'll need to buy some 'tea'.

Attendant: You're in the right place. We're right next to the Tea section. *(Indicates)* I'll leave you to it.

Student: Tea. That's got to be pretty straightforward. I mean, how many different choices can there be?

(STUDENT gazes up and down the tea section, getting increasingly frustrated, sighing, consulting the list)

Attendant: You OK?

Student: Yes. I think I've narrowed it down to a choice of Organic Cleanse Tea, Instant Lemon Reduced Sweetness Tea, Hard Water Loose Leaf Tea, or Crisp and Crunchy Traditional Pickled Onions in a Jar.

Reproduced with permission from *Drama out of a Crisis*, BRF 2012 (978 0 85746 005 9) www.barnabasinchurches.org.uk

Attendant: I think the last item has been mis-shelved. It's not really 'tea' in the traditional sense.

Student: Oh, this is hopeless. (*Ripping up the list in frustration*) All I want is a nice, relaxing, comforting cup of hot tea.

Attendant: OK. Let's narrow it down to 'ordinary' tea. In bags. Do you want a branded item or supermarket own?

Student: (*Distressed*) I don't know!

Attendant: OK, OK. Supermarket ones are cheaper. Is that OK? (*STUDENT nods, sobbing a little*) There. 40 ordinary tea bags. (*Gives to STUDENT*)

Student: Thank you. (*Examines packet*) What's this symbol?

Attendant: That's the Unfair trademark.

Student: Unfair trade?

Attendant: Ignore that. It's something they're made to put on the packet. Just buy it and don't worry about it.

Student: But it says here that the Unfair trade mark guarantees that poor farmers are given an unfair and unstable price for their products.

Attendant: (*Cheery*) Yes, and it keeps the prices down.

Student: And that unfair trade ensures that farmers and estate workers have no way of improving their lives. They work for minimal wages and struggle to feed themselves and their families. Their children are far less likely to go to school.

Attendant: Despite all that, it makes a surprisingly average cup of tea.

Reproduced with permission from *Drama out of a Crisis*, BRF 2012 (978 0 85746 005 9) www.barnabasinchurches.org.uk

Student: Isn't there an alternative?

Attendant: Yes. There's coffee. And there are plenty of other unfair products to choose from—chocolate, wine, bananas, sugar, honey, peanuts, cotton, flowers…

Student: And if I buy all those, I'll keep people locked in poverty?

Attendant: Guaranteed.

Student: Well, thank you very much, but I'm not prepared to pay to keep people in poverty. I'd prefer to pay a little more and give people a livelihood and a future. I'm taking my business elsewhere. *(Picks up mobile)* Mum, I don't like this kind of shopping. It's surprisingly nasty. Can you come and rescue me?

END

Reproduced with permission from *Drama out of a Crisis*, BRF 2012 (978 0 85746 005 9) www.barnabasinchurches.org.uk

*

Governance and corruption

Mind your own business

Curtain up

Good governance is essential to releasing people from poverty,
but its huge potential is lost when governments fulfil self-centred
ambitions rather than the needs and priorities of the people they
serve.

An effective and accountable government, engaged by a vibrant
civil society, can be a catalyst for development and enable millions
of people to flourish. It's a win–win situation: life improves, and
confidence in public institutions is enhanced, creating a peaceful
and secure environment for everyone.

Bible backdrop

They promise freedom, but they themselves are slaves of sin and
corruption. For you are a slave to whatever controls you.
2 PETER 2:19 (NLT)

We all understand corruption as something that spreads and taints.
When it happens on a large scale, permitted, overlooked or even
indulged by those in authority, it can be devastating, particularly to
the poorest people in society.

Sermon prompt

In Genesis 37—50 we see the story of Joseph, an amazing example of a godly servant who refused to be corrupted. Joseph's story is also a testimony to how good governance can save people from an imminent catastrophe, such as the effects of famine, which were averted by Joseph's advanced planning and care for the people of Egypt.

It might be a good opportunity to challenge people about how they can be prone to corruption in their lives. Little things such as illegally downloading films, 'borrowing' stationery from work, or doing the weekly shop online in office hours, can grow and lead to bigger corruption.

Taking it further: Campaign against injustice

Tearfund's 'Unearth the Truth' campaign aims to force mining, oil and gas companies to publish what they pay to developing country governments in order to access a country's resources. The campaign calls for transparency, not secrecy, from these industries in their dealings with the governments of developing countries. To learn more about 'Unearth the Truth' and join the campaign, visit www. tearfund.org/unearth. Here you can find details of forthcoming events and statistics about corruption, and access resources to engage your church.

Cast

There are three cast members, INTERVIEWER 1, INTERVIEWER 2 and CANDIDATE, all of whom can be male or female.

Staging: props, costumes and effects

All three characters wear smart work suits, but CANDIDATE should look particularly smart for the big day. All you need are a few chairs but, if you want to go further, you could have a laptop and a presentation projected on to a screen.

Script: Mind your own business

Shady dealing unfairly secures future employment, but at what cost?

Scene

CANDIDATE is facing a panel of two INTERVIEWERS, who are asleep, snoring.

Candidate: *(Standing, confident)* I have the streamlined capacity to get on-message about your dot-com monitored mobility, and my upgraded business approach model offers balanced logistical flexibility, particularly if you're going forward with plans to implement total incremental contingencies. *(Beat)* So, in summary, those are the 37 main and 68 supplementary reasons why I am the ideal candidate for your job. *(Sits)*

(INTERVIEWERS 1 and 2 wake up with a jolt)

Interviewer 1: *(Still half asleep)* Can I have runny eggs and soldiers, Darling Sweetie Pie?
Candidate: Pardon?
Interviewer 1: *(Waking)* Sorry, I must have drifted off… Where were we?
Interviewer 2: I think we were drawing the interview to a close.
Interviewer 1: Thank goodness.

Interviewer 2: We do have one final question…

Interviewer 1: *(Under his breath)* Yeah, do you ever shut up?

Candidate: Sorry?

Interviewer 2: Where do you see yourself in five years' time?

Interviewer 1: *(To INTERVIEWER 2)* If the answer is the same length as the last one, we'll still be trapped in this room.

Candidate: Pardon?

Interviewer 1: I was just wondering if you could make your final answer a little more succinct. I don't want to leave this interview to find that the apes have taken over Planet Earth.

Interviewer 2: So, where do you see yourself in five years' time?

Candidate: I'll keep it brief. I'd like to be on a hill, maybe, eating grass.

Interviewer 2: *(Surprised)* It's not really the answer we were looking for. That's where you see yourself in five years' time? On a hill..?

Interviewer 1: Eating grass? It doesn't… make any sense.

Candidate: I do have a much fuller explanation, but it might take a bit of a while to go through in detail…

Interviewer 1: No, that's fine, we'll work it out.

Interviewer 2: Thank you very much for what has been an extraordinary interview.

Candidate: Really? I thought it went rather badly from the start.

Interviewer 1: Yes, your opening handshake was quite hearty.

Interviewer 2: Thank you for waiting while my colleague was rushed to A&E.

Candidate: How are the old pinkies?

Interviewer 1: *(Tries to move his hand)* Still struggling to grip a pen. But the X-ray showed it was only a hairline fracture.

Candidate: Then there was my nosebleed. It's a nervous thing…

Interviewer 2: All over our sandwiches…

Candidate: The fruit will wipe clean, though. *(Remembering)* And I've no idea how I got my tie caught in my flies.

Interviewer 1: Your flies. My tie.

Candidate: Crumbs, yes. So, after all that, what are my chances of getting the job?

Interviewer 1: We've seen a number of strong candidates, and it's going to be a very tough decision.

Interviewer 2: Extremely hard to pick one person out over another.

Interviewer 1: That's why we wanted to ask if you had anything *else* you'd like to offer.

Interviewer 2: Something, perhaps, that you could give to us to…

Interviewer 1: … smooth the process a little.

Interviewer 2: Something that might *reward* us, and make us more likely to choose you above the others.

Candidate: I'm not sure I'm clear what you mean.

Interviewer 1: Something you could give to us, no questions asked, that we could take away and say no more about it.

Candidate: I'm still not quite getting it.

Interviewer 2: *(Clears his throat)* We take cash or cheque.

Interviewer 1: Credit or debit card. But not Switch.

Candidate: Are you expecting a bribe?

Interviewer 2: No. No. No. *(Laughs)*

Interviewer 1: No. No. No. *(Joins laughter)*

Interviewer 2: Actually, yes. If you are generous enough, the job is yours.

Candidate: That's remarkably simple.

Interviewer 1: And it means you don't have to be any good at the job.

Candidate: Perfect. I'll pay by credit card, please.

Interviewer 2: That'll do nicely. *(Takes card)*

Candidate: What a brilliant system. Instead of being good at stuff, you can just pay to get ahead. Suits me.

Interviewer 2: It seems to work. *(Hands over card in machine)*

Candidate: It's good for everyone. *(Enters PIN)* Good for me. Good for you.

Interviewer 2: Oh, it's great for us. *(Hands card back to CANDIDATE)*

Candidate: Fantastic.

Interviewer 1: And if you just remember to bring some form of payment along with you every day.

Candidate: Every day?

Interviewer 2: You want to get on, don't you?

Interviewer 1: Get a good appraisal?

Interviewer 2: Get that promotion?

Interviewer 1: Keep hold of your pension?

Candidate: Yes. But I didn't think...

Interviewer 1: See you Monday. I told you it was good for us.

END

Reproduced with permission from *Drama out of a Crisis*, BRF 2012 (978 0 85746 005 9) www.barnabasinchurches.org.uk

*

Speaking out

How to achieve your ultimate dream through the power of you

Curtain up

The church is called to speak out on behalf of and alongside people who have no voice. It's not that poor communities around the world can't speak for themselves; it's more that their voices simply aren't heard or, worse, they're ignored. Each of us has a different role to play but we must all work together to prevent the damage caused by injustices around the world.

Bible backdrop

Speak up for those who cannot speak for themselves, for the rights of all who are destitute.
PROVERBS 31:8 (NIV)

By campaigning for justice, we obey the biblical principle of speaking up for people who are facing extreme hardship. God calls on each of us to stand up against injustice and to find ways in which we can get involved.

Sermon prompt

As this sketch takes its inspiration from the book of Jonah, it would be good to accompany it with reflections from the story of that minor prophet. There may be many people like Jonah in your congregation, people who would prefer to flee to the sea than speak out against injustice. But the Bible demonstrates that God calls all of us to challenge unfair practices and shows that he will equip us even if we feel unable to speak up (see also the story of Moses, especially Exodus 3:7–12).

Taking it further: Speak up

One of the major concerns that people have is that they're not equipped: they simply don't know enough about the problems. Thankfully, Tearfund and other campaigning organisations offer simple and achievable actions that everyone can take, such as sending a quick postcard to your MP, joining campaign rallies and lobbying events. If you're on Facebook or have an iPhone, Tearfund provides a brilliant digital campaigning tool called Super Badger. Find out more about all of this and how you can get involved at www.tearfund.org/campaigning.

Cast

This is a dramatic monologue, so there's only one cast member, JONAH, who the Bible specifies is male. Learning lines is always best but, if time is tight, the script can be read openly, as it is supposed to be a speech.

Staging: props, costumes and effects

Not much staging is required (JONAH could simply stand at a lectern) but you could provide him with a PowerPoint and projector to accompany his presentation. JONAH should be groomed and sharp-suited, like the smiling life coaches who adorn those now-ubiquitous self-help books.

Script: How to achieve your ultimate dream through the power of you

Minor prophet Jonah offers his top tips on how to run a successful advocacy campaign.

Scene

To great applause, JONAH enters the stage, composes himself and begins, confidently.

Jonah: Thank you, ladies and gentlemen—or should I say, 'winners' and 'succeeders'. I know 'succeeders' isn't, strictly speaking, a word, but we all know what it means.

As the 156th speaker in a series of talks about how you can achieve your ultimate dream, I'm here today to tell you that you don't need to change your life in any way. Yes, nothing about you needs to change. Sure, you're depressed. Yes, you're an outcast. Fine, nobody's interested in pathetic old 'you'. But don't waste your life trying to improve yourself. It's the world that needs to change, friend, not you. You're OK just as you are.

Reproduced with permission from *Drama out of a Crisis,* BRF 2012 (978 0 85746 005 9) www.barnabasinchurches.org.uk

You can read about my amazing story in my latest book, *How to achieve your ultimate dream through the power of you*, but I'd like to pick out the salient points for your being a successful world-changer. *(Beat)* Like me.

The first incredible thing that happened to me was when God told me to go to a land far away, a dangerous debauched place where the laws were unjust and the rulers corrupt. I did what any right-thinking person would do when faced with a clear directive from the Almighty. Yes, I panicked and ran away, which brings me to rule number one in how to be a world-changer: always do the exact opposite of what God says.

I found a boat heading in the opposite direction, climbed on board and hid. Now I know God is omnipotent, omniscient and omnipresent, but I thought, if I wore a false moustache, donned a sailor's hat and kept my head down, he'd overlook the fact that I should be somewhere else entirely. But oh no, not God—next thing I knew, the boat was rocked by a mighty wind. Pretty soon the sailors worked out that I was the cause of the intemperate tempest so they threw me overboard, which brings me to rule number two on the road to ultimate success: if you are certain to drown in rough seas, get yourself swallowed by a gigantic sea creature baying for blood.

There I was in the stomach of this expansive *poisson*. I wasn't having what you would call a 'whale of a time'. For three days I was trapped in its belly with little air, surrounded by rotting sea matter, pondering my actions. That's when I realised the error of my ways and prayed. Actually, the first thing I did was to try every conceivable way to extricate myself from the predicament using my own limited and frankly useless resources. Following 72 hours of utter failure to escape, I panicked again and turned to the Lord for help.

God was clearly impressed by my eventual penitence—so much so that he kindly arranged for the giant fish to vomit me on to dry land. I awoke covered in whale bile, rotting halibut and diced carrots, only to realise that God had stranded me directly on the dreaded land I was attempting to avoid. That brings me to rule number three: whatever you do, don't trust God. He's crafty.

Once on *terra firma*, I was ready to flee to the hills but God kept bringing up my recent remorse and insisted I head for the palace of my enemies. So, reeking like the inside of a prehistoric sea serpent, I set off for Nineveh. I thought, God's no fool, he'll have caused me to be puked up somewhere within a short stroll of the king of Nineveh's castle. Yeah, right.

Three agonising sun-scorched days later, I finally caught sight of the palatial pad.

Rule number four is this: if you're going to be vomited up ahead of a state visit, bring some suntan lotion and aftershave to mask the stench. I didn't.

Anyway, surprisingly, my blood-and-thunder speech, calling on the people of Nineveh to repent, went down rather well. The king decreed that everyone should give up their wicked ways—and they did, just like that.

Well, you can imagine my reaction. I was furious. God showed pity, mercy and extended grace towards these people. How incredibly annoying is that?

The story goes on a bit more but I won't bore you with the whole 'giant plant, worm eating giant plant' incident. Suffice to say that if I, Jonah, can be a world-changer, then anyone can—even you lot. So please ignore rules one to four, because there's only one point to make: if God asks you to speak out against injustice, you'd better watch out. He's perfectly capable of using you to change the world. *(Beat)* Whether you like it or not.

END

Reproduced with permission from *Drama out of a Crisis*, BRF 2012 (978 0 85746 005 9) www.barnabasinchurches.org.uk

*

Church mobilisation

Every grain of sand

Curtain up

Church mobilisation is simply getting local churches to be proactive in responding to the needs of the community around them. The process starts with training local church ministers to help them learn, through Bible study, that Jesus' call is to offer the whole gospel to people—material and spiritual life transformation. Once ministers have caught this vision, they can instil it into their congregations.

Bible backdrop

How precious to me are your thoughts, God! How vast is the sum of them! Were I to count them, they would outnumber the grains of sand.
PSALM 139:17–18 (NIV)

We have much to learn from God, and one valuable lesson is that he wants us to work together. Jesus built his church (literally 'a gathering') as a force for transformation, because by working together, sharing skills and knowledge, we can be much more effective.

Sermon prompt

This sketch is for children but it's lots of fun so it would work in an all-age setting. It tells the story of three people who all have a gift but who need to come together and share what they have in order to do something greater. God has many great ideas and he shares with us his wisdom, but we don't always use our knowledge and resources wisely.

It would be up to the speaker to make the connection with issues of poverty. How can we join together to offer a more effective response to people who are suffering around the world and those suffering on our doorstep? Also, how can we help to equip churches, or offer encouragement to churches to use their own resources, in the poorest places on the earth?

Taking it further

Talk about how Jesus has brought us together as a church. We should share what we have—our talents, our gifts and all the things we own. As a church we can do many things that we wouldn't be able to do by ourselves. When we are church together, it is much better than being on our own. Explore the fact that there are many churches across the world with whom we can also join together, and that we, who have plenty, can help those who have very little.

Cast

There are four cast members: ONE, TWO, THREE and FOUR. All parts could be played by males or females.

Staging: props, costumes and effects

You'll definitely need a seaside bucket and spade and some sand for this sketch. It would be good also to spread out a plastic sheet to catch the sand.

Script: Every grain of sand

Three frustrated people join together and share their skills, thanks to a fourth.

Scene

Three people come together to form a line on stage. ONE carries a small seaside spade, TWO has a seaside bucket and THREE goes to stand next to a small pile of damp sand.

One: (*Holding spade*) What a great piece of design. A handle and a scoop, all you need to get digging. So that's what I'll do. (*ONE attempts to dig the floor, but it's too hard*) Oh dear. It's not really made for digging hard floors. (*Tries again, but no better. Tries to balance the spade on nose: it falls off with a clatter*) Oh, this is useless. (*Kicks the spade in disgust*)

Two: (*To ONE*) Don't be so cross. Just because you're jealous of my lovely bucket. Oh yes. (*Admiring*) It's wonderful. A firm base. No holes. Brilliant. (*Looks again*) Not sure what it's for, though. (*Puts bucket on the floor and tries to sit on it. Falls off, picks it up again, pops it on head*) Who turned out the lights? (*Wanders off and bumps into THREE*)

Three: You clumsy twit! Watch where you're going. (*Takes TWO's bucket. TWO shouts out in alarm*

	when he sees THREE) You nearly trod all over my lovely sand. *(Running hand through it)* Lovely, lovely sand. It's good for… standing on. *(Stands on the sand)* Yes and… *(Thinks)* exfoliating the skin. *(Rubs some on face)* And… *(pause)* lots of other stuff… Can't think of any myself.
One:	Sand? Useless. What's the point of sand?
Three:	So I can put it on my head and walk into things? No thanks. I'm happy with sand, thank you.
One:	Oh yes, 'cos sand is so great. What can you do with sand?
Two:	More than you can do with that stupid spade.
Three:	You've dug yourself into a right hole, there!
One:	Well, I'm sticking with my spade, thank you.
Two:	And I'll keep my bucket, thanks.
Three:	Then I'll hold on to my sand, if you please.

(They carry on trying to do things with their items. All of them fail. ONE, then TWO, then THREE all get fed up and sit down in a huff. FOUR enters and looks at all of them)

Four:	What are you lot up to?
One, Two and Three:	Nothing.
Four:	*(To ONE)* Is that your spade?
One:	Yes, but it's useless.
Four:	*(Moving to TWO)* Is that your bucket?
Two:	This bucket? I might as well throw it in the bin.
Four:	*(Moving to THREE)* And yours is the sand?
Three:	You take it. It's rubbish.

Four:	You silly people. You haven't made any sandcastles at all!
One, Two and Three:	Sandcastles?
One:	Don't be daft…
Two:	We can't make sandcastles…
Three:	How can we make sandcastles?
Four:	You've got everything you need right here. (To ONE) You pick up your spade. (To TWO) You bring your bucket. (To THREE) And you gather some sand. (They do as asked) By joining together and sharing all you have, you can do far more than you can on your own.
One, Two and Three:	Thank you!
One:	Each of us has something to help us make sandcastles. But what do you have?
Four:	I don't have anything.
Two:	Oh yes you do!
Three:	You were the one who helped us to join together.
One:	Yes, you are the most important of all.
Two:	Come and join us and help us to make sandcastles!

(FOUR joins with the others)

END

Reproduced with permission from *Drama out of a Crisis*, BRF 2012 (978 0 85746 005 9) www.barnabasinchurches.org.uk

*

Church and community mobilisation

We are church

Curtain up

Tearfund upholds church and community mobilisation as the best and most sustainable method of development. When churches fully grasp and put into practice the fullness of the gospel—transformation in all aspects of life—they can use their unique position in communities to be a catalyst for huge and lasting transformation.

'The process told us we cannot wait for someone to come, we are to be salt and light in the world... and it helped us to understand that we had many resources to help ourselves,' says Pastor Ezra from Uganda.

Through church and community mobilisation, churches can encourage and empower communities to meet their own needs. The ultimate aim is that communities will no longer need outside help or, at least, will need a much reduced level of support. This will mean that the support they used to depend on can be used to start the process with other communities.

Bible backdrop

'I will build my church, and death itself will not have any power over it.'
MATTHEW 16:18

What good is the church? When considering some parts of the church today, this is a very pertinent question. Yet Jesus saw his church as a powerful, unstoppable force for transformation and growth. When local churches are activated to meet the needs of poor and oppressed people, they discover the fullness of God's calling.

Sermon prompt

This sketch may surprise some people because it challenges a widespread perception of what development is and how we can meet the needs of poor communities. I have been privileged to hear about and witness first-hand the amazing transformation that occurs when churches and communities are mobilised. The most impressive part is how self-sufficient poor communities can become, once they are empowered to realise that they have resources and skills.

The sketch is based on a true story told to me by a church pastor from Tearfund's partner, Eagles Relief and Development, when I visited them in Malawi in 2009. Of course, I've exaggerated it for comic effect, but it's strangely true.

Taking it further: Discovery course

A partnership started by Tearfund and Livability, Community Mission encourages churches to put faith into action and to offer the fullness of the gospel—integral mission—to the communities around them.

'Discovery' is a practical process from Tearfund, as part of Community Mission, that is designed to help your church become a transforming influence in your community. Written by skilled practitioners with extensive experience of working in inner-city communities, Discovery draws on Tearfund's expertise in working with churches and community groups overseas and in the UK. The aim of Discovery is to take the vision and strength of a church and help them to put their plans into action.

To learn more about Discovery, visit the Community Mission website: www.communitymission.org.uk.

Cast

This sketch has seven cast members: WORKER and BENEFICIARIES 1–6. The larger-than-usual cast is so that the sketch communicates the scale of the church and builds a momentum (like the church and community mobilisation process).

Staging: props, costumes and effects

You will need a big sack and a few props. From my experience, many poor communities in Africa wear similar clothes to yours and mine, but perhaps not as smart as you or I can afford and maintain. The important thing is not to give a clichéd impression of poor communities; the butt of the joke should remain the WORKER.

Script: We are church

Well-meaning aid worker is confronted with a nightmare scenario, a village that is self-sufficient.

Scene

A village in Africa. WORKER is on the phone; BENEFICIARY is nearby and comes closer during WORKER's next speech. Over the course of the sketch, more and more people from the village crowd around. (If you want to have more speaking parts, give some of BENEFICIARY's lines to others: see the numbers for suggestions.)

Worker: *(Dragging a big sack, on satellite phone)* I've just been helicoptered over. Then I leapt into a 4x4 and drove to this remote village—seven hours from civilisation. 18 hours from a Starbucks. Now I'm ready to feed the world.

(WORKER sees BENEFICIARY)

Worker: Got to go, just spotted my first beneficiary. Hello, Beneficiary. I'm here from Global Aid Incorporated. And you just got lucky—I'm here to drag you out of poverty. *(BENEFICIARY looks unimpressed)* Sorry, do you speak English?

Beneficiary 1: I do.

Worker: Thank goodness, because I don't speak a word of… whatever language it is you lot speak. Um. My friend.

Beneficiary 1: Have you just arrived?

Worker: I'm still a bit jet-lagged, to tell you the truth. Flew in today. Sorry, this is probably a bit beyond your understanding. (*Speaking slowly, using actions*) I came here from far, far away. I flew here on a giant metal bird. Zoom, zoom.

Beneficiary 2: An aeroplane, yes. Would you like something to eat?

Worker: Thanks. I'm absolutely starving. Oh, sorry. Little bit inappropriate. In fact, I have something for you. (*Shows big sack of 'dried meal'*) Ta-da!

Beneficiary 1: What is it?

Worker: Well, as it says, it's dried... meal. Which I'm sure is, um, delicious.

Beneficiary 2: You cook it?

Worker: Yes, just add... water. Oh. Do you have water?

Beneficiary 1: (*Examining the sack*) You eat this?

Worker: No, no, no. I wouldn't touch the stuff. There's a chef back at the compound. He's doing us a full English breakfast tomorrow. So we won't feel so homesick. This, my little beneficiary, is for you—and your village. It's what we call 'overseas aid'.

Beneficiary 2: Thank you. I'm sure we can empty it out and use the bag for something... (*Goes to pick it up*)

Worker: Oh, you can't just take it. You have to earn it. We don't want you to sit here lazily expecting us to drop off food whenever you get hungry.

Beneficiary 3: But we work every day, farming the fields, from when we wake until when the sun goes down.

Reproduced with permission from *Drama out of a Crisis*, BRF 2012 (978 0 85746 005 9) www.barnabasinchurches.org.uk

Worker: Then how would you like to earn yourself some dried meal?

Beneficiary 1: What are you asking us to do?

Worker: Education is vital: you're never going to get out of poverty if you're not educated. How about you build me a school?

Beneficiary 2: But we already have a school.

Worker: Oh, that's unfortunate. What about a well?

Beneficiary 3: There are many in the village.

Worker: Really? What about toilet blocks?

Beneficiary 4: We have our own toilets here.

Worker: What, these little mud huts? Don't you want brick toilets and flush loos? We could send a response team in…

Beneficiary 1: These are our toilets. We build as a community, one for each home. Then we can clean and maintain them using the resources around us.

Worker: What about a road? Transport links are vital if you want to develop. A good road could transform this poor village.

Beneficiary 2: How did you arrive here?

Worker: My driver brought me.

Beneficiary 3: In a car?

Worker: Yes.

Beneficiary 4: On a road?

Worker: Yes.

Beneficiary 5: We have a road. The community came together to build it, as part of the community plan.

Worker: You know about the Community Plan?

Beneficiary 1: We do.

Reproduced with permission from *Drama out of a Crisis*, BRF 2012 (978 0 85746 005 9) www.barnabasinchurches.org.uk

Worker: But I haven't told you what it is yet. I wrote it back in my office in London. We did a remote needs assessment.

Beneficiary 2:   Our community came together and we discussed what we needed. Can we see your plan?

Worker: We'll be sending a team here soon. You can see it when we've finished.

Beneficiary 2:   But there are hundreds of villages here. Are you going to send a team to every one?

Worker: Oh, this is hopeless. I've got to get back to the compound before sundown. I'm told it's dangerous out here at night. Do you want this sack of food or what?

Beneficiary 4:   Not really. We have a cooperative here and we grow our own food. It is a struggle and the harvest is not always plentiful, but we are helping ourselves. We have been learning to farm better, to use drought-resistant crops.

Worker: All very enterprising, I'm sure, but what you don't understand is that I come from Global Aid Incorporated. We have offices in more than 15 countries.

Beneficiary 5:   Our organisation has millions of branches in every country in the world.

Worker: But we have a 20-year track record of delivering aid to the poor.

Beneficiary 6:   We have a 2000-year history of welcoming the poorest and most needy people into our community and transforming their whole lives.

Worker: Who are you?

Reproduced with permission from *Drama out of a Crisis*, BRF 2012 (978 0 85746 005 9) www.barnabasinchurches.org.uk

Crowd: We are the local church.

Beneficiary 2: We show communities the natural resources they have.

Beneficiary 3: We encourage individuals to believe in themselves because they are loved and valued.

Beneficiary 4: We help people to help themselves, and we know what a community needs because we are part of the community.

Beneficiary 5: We still struggle and we need support.

Beneficiary 6: But we have experts here in our own country who help us and train us. That is what we need. Why don't you help to provide them?

Worker: Sounds like there's one thing you don't need.

Beneficiary 1: What's that?

Worker: Some twit with a giant sack of dried meal.

END

Reproduced with permission from *Drama out of a Crisis,* BRF 2012 (978 0 85746 005 9) www.barnabasinchurches.org.uk

*

The Bible and poverty

Always with you

Curtain up

God cares deeply about poverty and justice—so much so that poverty is mentioned more than 2000 times in the Bible. Nearly every page of scripture demonstrates God's passion for poor and marginalised people, his compassion for the oppressed and his call for justice.

Bible backdrop

There will always be poor people in the land. Therefore I command you to be open-handed toward those of your people who are poor and needy in your land.
DEUTERONOMY 15:11 (TNIV)

Not only does God recognise how widespread and long-term poverty is in this age, but he also calls on his people to act generously to support and uphold people who are suffering through its effects. Poverty is an unmistakable fact across large parts of the world (and often on our own doorsteps), but how often do we choose to ignore it?

Sermon prompt

This is a tough sketch. It juxtaposes some of our idle thoughts and excuses about poverty—some expressed, some unacknowledged—with verses in the Bible that express God's response to poverty and his call on his people to take action. Lenny Bruce, a controversial American comedian, once said, 'Anyone who has two coats while someone else has none is not a true Christian.' Now that's challenging.

Taking it further: Integral mission

'Integral mission' is a phrase developed in Latin America around 30 years ago, but it does not describe anything new. It is the way of life that Jesus exemplified and called us to follow.

At its most basic, Integral Mission simply means 'having it all'. We want to worship and pray and preach and witness and serve and care. God put these things together and we should never have let them become separated.
MICAH DECLARATION ON INTEGRAL MISSION

The Integral Mission Initiative has set up a website offering resources such as podcasts, videos, articles and blogs that explore integral mission. If you want to delve deeper into integral mission and learn how to live it, visit www.integralmission.net.

Cast

There are only two speaking parts, ONE and TWO, who can be male or female.

Staging: props, costumes and effects

I haven't offered much in the way of stage directions because
I would like you to find a way to perform the sketch effectively.
Spend some time thinking about direction, but keep things simple
so that the words are heard and understood.

Script: Always with you

The Bible confronts poverty prejudices.

Scene

Arrange ONE and TWO across the performance area.

One: They're lazy, aren't they? I have to feed my family; they should, too.

Two: God will bless people who are poor.

One: They should pray more, follow Jesus... You've got to ask yourself, why are they in that position in the first place?

Two: God has given a great faith to those in need.

One: I don't like to look at them when I'm coming home in the dark. They're scary, and it upsets me.

Two: The Lord defends the homeless.

One: It's oppressive governments and corrupt regimes that keep people in that position.

Two: You must defend those who are helpless.

One: It's not like I'm rich. What can I give that will make any difference?

Two: Sell what you have and give the money to those in need.

One: With all these cutbacks and tax rises, I'm struggling to get things for myself, let alone give stuff away.

Two: If you have food, share it with someone else.

Reproduced with permission from *Drama out of a Crisis*, BRF 2012 (978 0 85746 005 9) www.barnabasinchurches.org.uk

One: I know this will sound a bit selfish, but what's in it for me?

Two: The Lord blesses everyone who freely gives.

One: It's not like I'm a bad person. I'm always welcoming people into my home.

Two: When you give a dinner or a banquet, invite those who cannot pay you back.

One: The reality is, I like being comfortable.

Two: Give money to those in need and you will have riches in heaven.

One: But I work hard and I deserve a reward right now, don't I?

Two: You have already had an easy life.

One: There's a lot wrong with this country that needs fixing before we can fix the world.

Two: Help those in need.

One: It's just not my calling. I don't get excited about it. Other people do. I'll leave it to them. It's their thing.

Two: Care about the rights of those in need.

One: Before I love others, I've got to learn to love myself. I've got a lot of things in my own life that I need God to sort out.

Two: If you won't help others, don't expect to be heard when you cry out for help.

One: I love God and I'm faithful to him. Isn't that enough?

Two: If we see one of our own people in need, we must have pity on that person, or else we cannot say we love God.

Reproduced with permission from *Drama out of a Crisis*, BRF 2012 (978 0 85746 005 9) www.barnabasinchurches.org.uk

One: I believe money and success are blessings from God. If God is blessing me, why should I give it away?

Two: The love of money causes all kinds of trouble.

One: OK, I know I'm supposed to give stuff away. Just don't expect me to like it.

Two: God loves people who love to give.

One: I know that we're supposed to be generous, but it's never really worked, right? People are just too selfish to live that way.

Two: All the Lord's followers shared everything they had.

One: It's not like I don't care—I do. I hope all goes well for them. I hope that they stay warm and have plenty to eat.

Two: I was hungry, but you did not give me anything to eat, and I was thirsty, but you did not give me anything to drink.

One: I know it's not the answer but I find it so hard when I hear about it or see it. When it comes on the news, I turn over. It's upsetting.

Two: You will always have those in need with you. (*Pause*) Always.

END

Reproduced with permission from *Drama out of a Crisis,* BRF 2012 (978 0 85746 005 9) www.barnabasinchurches.org.uk

*

And finally...

By way of a final word, I'd like to end with a poem written by a good friend of mine, Alex Mowbray. When I was gathering thoughts and ideas for this book, I thought of Alex, who writes amazing, challenging poetry. I asked him to offer his reflections on the stigma that many people living with HIV have to suffer. I thought he might provide me with something special—and he has...

Stigma? What stigma?

You have to look to find it here;
it might be on your street
hidden
for the sake of other people's fear.
Most of us don't really know,
we'd rather not,
one of life's unpleasant facts.
Of course we've heard things,
seen a documentary
but never had to face them in the flesh.
What would we do?
Is there protocol, you know, procedures,
guidelines for our interaction? After all
it's good to be prepared.
Dare we shake a naked hand?
How about a hug, a kiss?
From what we've heard
it's safer just to give the intimate a miss.
Apparently you carry HIV for years

suppressed by drugs and counselling
until your energy runs out
but if your skin erupts in boils and sores
you just can't hide it any more.

Full-blown AIDS:
what prejudice in those few words:
not just the devastation or the pain,
the anguish and relentless symptoms...
it's the isolation, separation,
the increasing powerlessness.
What does one say?
'I'm sorry' sounds inadequate.
You ask them how they're feeling and they ask you
if you really want to know.
You don't.
You do.
You're curious;
a person just like you is hosting killer bugs in healthy cells
that gain complete immunity.
Ironic isn't it?
You wish them all the best, of course,
avoiding platitudes while thanking God
you're not like one of them.
They would get out more if they could,
out of their bodies, trade them in
for anything but torturous departure
of their colleagues and their friends.
Gathered family with brave and desperate eyes
try not to cry.

Being human seems to mean we look for fault,
someone to blame.
Not that we cast first stone

but on the other hand
we're asking questions silently…
shared needles, drugs or dodgy sex perhaps?
Does judgment ration sympathy?
They can read your face,
whose side you're on
after you've gone
leaving them alone.
Always alone.
Sometimes though the truth gets out
over the fence or through the school's gate…
respected to rejected in the whisper of a word.
Their kids ignored,
the looks and look-aways,
anger sprayed on windows,
faeces through the letterbox
and long, long uncertain days.

At least it's better here than over there
in Africa
where stigma bites deeper than mosquitoes,
where your secret's never safe for long,
where when you lose your job
you'll never get another one,
where treatment is available for some,
where sickness has no Benefit,
where death brings orphans, hardship and
a badge of family shame.
The more sick you are the further the clinic,
the more stories you hear the more they are tragic;
where those in communities who struggle to cope
are deprived of their rights, of their voice, of their hope.
For a woman it's worse, obliged to carry the blame
for man's misdemeanours or a life on the game

and there's plenty out there who love to play God
with dispassionate dogma and judgmental tone
preaching punishment now for sins in the flesh
with a justified sentence of death.
It's the rumours and the whispering,
the tumours and the blistering
that make them feel so apart, so unclean;
infected,
detected,
inspected like a leper
languishing...

What do we care?
We're over here not over there.

Enjoyed

this book?

Write a review—we'd love to hear what you think.
Email: reviews@brf.org.uk

Keep up to date—receive details of our new books as they happen.
Sign up for email news and select your interest groups at:
www.brfonline.org.uk/findoutmore/

Follow us on Twitter @brfonline

By post—to receive new title information by post (UK only), complete the form below and post to: BRF Mailing Lists, 15 The Chambers, Vineyard, Abingdon, Oxfordshire, OX14 3FE

Your Details
Name _____
Address_____
_____
Town/City _____ Post Code _____
Email_____

Your Interest Groups (*Please tick as appropriate)	
☐ Advent/Lent	☐ Messy Church
☐ Bible Reading & Study	☐ Pastoral
☐ Children's Books	☐ Prayer & Spirituality
☐ Discipleship	☐ Resources for Children's Church
☐ Leadership	☐ Resources for Schools

Support your local bookshop
Ask about their new title information schemes.